6...  W9-AXS-651

With very best
regards!

Dick

GROUP COUNSELING AND THERAPY TECHNIQUES
IN SPECIAL SETTINGS

Publication Number 928

AMERICAN LECTURE SERIES®

A Publication In

The BANNERSTONE DIVISION of
AMERICAN LECTURES IN SOCIAL
AND REHABILITATION PSYCHOLOGY

Editors of the series

JOHN G. CULL, PH.D.
Director, Regional Counselor Training Program
Department of Rehabilitation Counseling
Virginia Commonwealth University
Fishersville, Virginia

and

RICHARD E. HARDY, ED.D.
Chairman, Department of Rehabilitation Counseling
Virginia Commonwealth University
Richmond, Virginia

The American Lecture Series in Social and Rehabilitation Psychology offers books which are concerned with man's role in his milieu. Emphasis is placed on how this role can be made more effective in a time of social conflict and a deteriorating physical environment. The books are oriented toward descriptions of what future roles should be and are not concerned exclusively with the delineation and definition of contemporary behavior. Contributors are concerned to a considerable extent with prediction through the use of a functional view of man as opposed to a descriptive, anatomical point of view.

Books in this series are written mainly for the professional practioner; however, the academician will find them of considerable value in both undergraduate and graduate courses in the helping services.

GROUP COUNSELING AND THERAPY TECHNIQUES IN SPECIAL SETTINGS

Richard E. Hardy, Ed.D.
John G. Cull, Ph.D.

CHARLES C THOMAS • PUBLISHER
Springfield • Illinois • U.S.A.

Published and Distributed Throughout the World by

CHARLES C THOMAS • PUBLISHER
Bannerstone House
301-327 Lawrence Avenue, Springfield, Illinois, U.S.A.

*With THOMAS BOOK careful attention is given to all details of
manufacturing and design. It is the Publisher's desire to present books
that are satisfactory as to their physical qualities and artistic possibilities
and appropriate for their particular use. THOMAS BOOKS will be
true to those laws of quality that assure a good name and good will.*

Printed in the United States of America
PP-22

Library of Congress Cataloging in Publication Data

Hardy, Richard E
    Group counseling and therapy techniques in special settings.
    (American lecture series, publication no. 928. A publication in the
Bannerstone division of American lectures in social and rehabilitation
psychology)
    1. Counseling—Addresses, essays, lectures.
2. Group psychotherapy—Addresses, essays ,lectures.
I. Cull, John G., joint author. II. Title.
[DNLM: 1. Counseling. 2. Psychotherapy, Group. WM430 H271g
1974]
BF637.C6H328   616.8'915   73-13992
ISBN 0-398-03001-4

CONTRIBUTORS

Kathryn H. Allan, M.A.: Social Science Research Analyst for the Social Security Administration. Co-author of a recent government report, "General Characteristics of the Disabled." Formerly, assistant director of a national study on drug-use, for The Johns Hopkins University, Baltimore, Maryland, and research coordinator for Project Know How, a program for disadvantaged families in Tallahassee, Florida. Ms. Allan has co-led many groups with her husband.

Thomas K. Allan, Ph.D.: Associate Professor of Education, Counseling and Personnel Services Department, and Coordinator of General Undergraduate Advisement, University of Maryland, College Park, Maryland. Presenter of APA paper, "Sensitivity Training of a Black/White Community Leader Group." Formerly, Assistant Professor of Counseling and Counseling Psychologist at Washington University, St. Louis, Missouri, and Florida State University, Tallahassee, Florida. Member of Division 17 of the American Psychological Association, Dr. Allan has led and co-led many groups of college students, the disadvantaged, and married couples.

John G. Cull, Ph.D.: Professor and Director, Regional Counselor Training Program, Department of Rehabilitation Counseling, Virginia Commonwealth University, Fishersville, Virginia; Adjunct Professor of Psychology and Education, School of General Studies, University of Virginia, Charlottesville, Virginia; Technical Consultant, Rehabilitation Services Administration, United States Department of Health, Education and Welfare, Washington, D.C.; Editor, American Lecture Series in Social and Rehabilitation Psychology, Charles C Thomas, Publisher; Lecturer Medical Department, Woodrow Wilson Rehabilitation Center; Formerly, Rehabilitation Counselor, Texas State Commission For The Blind; Rehabilitation Counselor, Texas Rehabilitation Commission; Director, Division of Research and Program Development, Virginia State Department of Vocational Rehabilitation. The following are some of the books which Dr. Cull has co-authored and co-edited: *Drug Dependence and Rehabilitation Approaches, Fundamentals of Criminal Behavior and Correctional Systems, Rehabilitation of the Drug Abuser With Delinquent Behavior,* and *Therapeutic Needs of the Family.* Dr. Cull has contributed more than fifty publications to the professional literature in psychology and rehabilitation.

Jack A. Duncan, Ed.D.: Associate Professor, Department of Counselor Education, Virginia Commonwealth University, Richmond, Virginia; former junior and senior high school teacher, high school counselor, and director of guidance; Director of Guidance and Testing, Board of Regents of the University System of Georgia; Editoria Board of *Counselor Education and Supervision;* Membership Chairman Designate of the National Vocational Guidance Association; and Member of the Association of Counselor Educators and Supervisors Commission on Women. Dr. Duncan's numerous publications have been addressed to a variety of areas in the field of guidance and counseling.

Richard E. Hardy, Ed.D.: Professor and Chairman, Department of Rehabilitation

Counseling, Virginia Commonwealth University, Richmond, Virginia; Technical Consultant, United States Department of Health, Education and Welfare, Rehabilitation Services Administration, Washington, D.C.; Editor, American Lecture Series in Social and Rehabilitation Psychology, Charles C Thomas, Publisher; and Associate Editor, *Journal of Voluntary Action Research,* formerly Rehabilitation Counselor in Virginia, Rehabilitation Advisor, Rehabilitation Services Administration, United States Department of Health, Education and Welfare, Washington, D.C., former Chief Psychologist and Supervisor of Professional Training, South Carolina Department of Rehabilitation and member of the South Carolina State Board of Examiners in Psychology. The following are some of the books which Dr. Hardy has co-authored and co-edited: *Drug Dependence and Rehabilitation Approaches, Fundamentals of Criminal Behavior and Correctional Systems, Rehabilitation of the Drug Abuser with Delinquent Behavior,* and *Therapeutic Needs of the Family.* Dr. Hardy has contributed more than fifty publications to the professional literature in psychology and rehabilitation.

Robert A. Lassiter, Ph.D.: Associate Professor, Department of Rehabilitation Counseling, School of Community Services, Virginia Commonwealth University; Technical Consultant, Rehabilitation Services Administration, Department of Health, Education and Welfare; Contributor, *American Lecture Series in Social and Rehabilitation Psychology,* Charles C Thomas, Publisher. Formerly, Rehabilitation Counselor, Florida Division of Vocational Rehabilitation, Executive Director, North Carolina Society for Crippled Children and Adults, State Director, North Carolina Division of Vocational Rehabilitation; Project Director, Rehabilitation Education and Research Unit, Rehabilitation Counseling Program, School of Education, University of North Carolina. Author of articles on vocational rehabilitation in professional, educational and rehabilitation journals.

Steven Mathew Ross, Ph.D.: Chief, Drug Dependence Treatment Center, V.A. Hospital, Salt Lake City, Utah; Instructor, Department of Psychiatry, University of Utah Medical Center, Salt Lake City, Utah; Assistant Clinical Professor, Department of Psychology, University of Utah. Formerly, Program Supervisor, Behavior Modification Training Center, Salt Lake City, Utah, and Staff Psychologist, V.A. Hospital, East Orange, New Jersey. Dr. Ross is very active in research which has led to a number of publications in psychological and psychogically oriented journals.

Joyce Testa Salhoot, M.S.W.: Instructor, Department of Physical Medicine and Rehabilitation, Baylor University College of Medicine, Houston, Texas; Assistant Director, Regional Spinal Cord Center, Texas Institute for Rehabilitation and Research; and Social Worker on the Spinal Cord Unit of the Texas Institute for Rehabilitation and Research. She has been active as a field instructor for the University of Houston Graduate School of Social Work. Mrs. Salhoot holds degrees from Niagara University in Niagara Falls, New York and Tulane University in New Orleans, Louisiana. She is a member of various professional organizations related to social work and rehabilitation.

This book is dedicated to three outstanding educators and practitioners

Dr. Richard H. Byrne, Professor
Counseling and Personnel Services
University of Maryland

Dr. Thomas M. Magoon
Professor of Psychology and Education
Director of the Counseling Center
University of Maryland

Dr. George L. Marx
Professor and Chairman of Counseling and Personnel Services
University of Maryland

The following books have appeared thus far in the Social and Rehabilitation Psychology Series:

PREFACE

This book was developed and completed only after a great deal of consideration had been given to the selection of the contributors and decisions had been made relative to the approaches which should be suggested to them in the development of their materials. The individuals who contributed to this book are outstanding individuals in their specialty areas. Not only are they well known in counseling but also they have great expertise in the special areas to which they have applied the group work techniques explained in each individual chapter and section.

The result of their efforts is that this book offers a great deal of practitioner oriented material on techniques which are useful with special populations. Group counseling has been shown to be especially useful in various settings and the purpose of this book is to pinpoint those settings and describe techniques and approaches in practical style. We owe a great deal to the contributors in that they have had to tolerate frequent phone calls, letters and criticisms which at times may have been inappropriate. Without their interest and close cooperation this book could never have been developed.

We feel that the book takes an unusual approach from the practitioner point of view in offering applications of group work with exceptional populations.

Richard E. Hardy
John G. Cull

Richmond, Virginia

CONTENTS

Contents

GROUP COUNSELING AND THERAPY TECHNIQUES IN SPECIAL SETTINGS

CHAPTER I

GROUP COUNSELING WITH ADOLESCENTS IN THE SCHOOL SETTING

JACK A. DUNCAN

INTRODUCTION

T HERE IS NO SINGLE counseling approach that is most effective for dealing with the concerns and problems of all adolescents. Some respond favorably to the more traditional one-to-one approach to counseling while others find a group setting to be more nearly appropriate for meeting their particular needs. It is also true that some counselors tend to work more effectively in a group setting than in a one-to-one relationship and demonstrate successes with individuals in groups that they do not show in the individual setting. Therefore, in this chapter I shall concentrate on the group approach for helping adolescents deal with their developmental concerns.

However, before I explore the group counseling technique, it will be necessary to define group counseling as it will be used in

3

this chapter. The most nearly comprehensive definition in the literature is that proposed by Gazda, Duncan, and Meadows (1967):

> Group counseling is a dynamic interpersonal process focusing on conscious thought and behavior and involving the therapy functions of permissiveness, orientation to reality, catharsis, and mutual trust, caring, understanding, acceptance, and support. The therapy functions are created and nurtured in a small group through the sharing of personal concerns with one's peers and the counselor(s). The group counselors are basically normal individuals with various concerns which are not debilitating to the extent requiring extensive personality change. The group counselees may utilize the group interaction to increase understanding and acceptance of values and goals and to learn and/or unlearn certain attitudes and behaviors. (p. 305)

The essence of this definition is that *group counseling* is growth-oriented; i.e., the projected outcomes of the group experience are intellectual, social, and emotional growth for the individual participant. Since group counseling is preventive-remedial in nature, it serves the dual purposes of preventing the development of problems or concerns for participants as well as remediating those that have already developed. (Throughout this chapter, the terms "problems" and "concerns" will be used interchangeably, although they do not have the same connotation for me.)

Another approach with respect to group procedures that merits clarification is group guidance. Much of the literature in the past and to some extent some contemporary sources have drawn distinctions between group counseling and group guidance. However, some authors have, through ignorance or indifference, used the terms interchangeably.

Group guidance, as used in this chapter, is defined as a procedure in which the primary emphasis is on the giving of information by a leader to an unlimited number of recipients with special emphasis on providing information in areas not covered by traditional curricula offerings; e.g., interpersonal relations, boy-girl relations, test interpretation, and school orientation. In essence, this is a task-oriented procedure, geared toward the giving and receiving of information within the group setting with little *conscious* concern directed toward *individual* growth as described in group counseling, although the concern for individual growth is included as part of the anticipated outcomes, and its importance is in no way minimzed.

Furthermore, group guidance is preventive in its orientation. One of the underlying assumptions is that by providing students information in areas with which they will need to deal in the process of growing and maturing many problems, conflicts, and concerns can be prevented.

One additional major group procedure, psychotherapy, needs to be reviewed here in order to put group work into some manageable perspective. Psychotherapy is a group procedure which traditionally deals with individuals in a group who have demonstrated some severe personality or character disorders and who meet over a period of time with a trained psychologist or psychiatrist, usually in an institutional setting, with one of the goals of the procedure being to bring about positive changes in the personalitites of the participants. The thrust of the technique is remedial.

Although most school counselors are trained and possess the skills to conduct group guidance sessions, and some are trained and skilled in group counseling techniques, it is extremely doubtful that even the most highly trained and experienced school counselors would ever possess the credentials prerequisite to undertaking group psychotherapy sessions. For a school counselor to propose or even suggest undertaking the responsibility for group psychotherapy sessions would not only be foolhardy and unethical but also dangerous to the participants.

No treatise on group counseling in the school setting would be complete without some reference to the recent dramatic and explosive emergence of a wide variety of disparate group procedures euphemistically referred to as the Human Potential Movement. The movement includes a multitude of "techniques," "approaches", and "games" which are designed to create an awareness within the individual that will enhance his overall level of effectiveness in dealing with himself, others, and his environment.

It is not within the purview of this chapter to explore even superficially these procedures, but it must be pointed out that a school counselor would be well advised to defer attempting to utilize these procedures—if in fact he would use them at all—until he has undergone extensive training under a qualified trainer in the theory and practice of the given procedure. There is, in fact, in some professional circles some question as to the ethical and moral consideration of utilizing these approaches with any group, let alone a group of junior or senior high school students.

Having reviewed briefly the three major group procedures—group counseling, group guidance, and group psychotherapy—and having referred to the Human Potential Movement, it would seem appropriate to provide a very brief overview of the historical development of group work.

SOME ORIGINS OF GROUP COUNSELING

The origin of group counseling as a technique employed in working with students is difficult to pinpoint. A review of the related literature depicts the development of group counseling as an amalgamation of a number of group techniques utilized by various social scientists as well as the medical profession. For example, the child study approach of Alfred Adler, the influences of group dynamics and Kurt Lewin, the guidance information sessions and homeroom guidance point of view of Ruth Strang, the psychodrama of J. L. Moreno, the early work in group counseling in the school setting of Merle Ohlsen, and the developmental group counseling of George Gazda have all contributed to the principles and practices of group counseling as we know it today.

It would be impossible to review in this chapter all the principles and practices of group counseling that have been developed and established through experience and research. Instead, I shall review what I feel are the essential considerations for establishing and conducting successful group counseling sessions. These considerations are the primary purposes of the group, advantages of the group, formation of the group, open and closed groups, homogeneity versus heterogeneity in group composition, group composition by sex, physical setting, duration of sessions, time and frequency of meeting, counselor's role, counselee's role, the first session, continuing group sessions, precautionary measures, and the final session.

PRIMARY PURPOSES OF THE GROUP

The primary purposes of the group and group counseling in

particular are: (1) to provide a learning experience for the participants that cannot be gained in any other way; (2) to provide help through peer support to adolescents with their developmental concerns; (3) to use the strengths of the group counseling technique to facilitate positive change in the lives of the adolescent participants; (4) to utilize the group as a vehicle through which adolescents can explore ways in which they can prevent problems from developing in their lives as they grow and mature; and (5) to use the group as a vehicle through which adolescents can receive help in resolving problems or concerns that they already have.

Another purpose often given by authorities in the field for forming counseling groups and upon which there does not seem to be consensus at this time is that of providing a means of reaching more students in a limited amount of time. The premise appears to be sound, but in actual practice it cannot always be supported. Gazda *et al.* (1967) in their survey, point out that some practitioners maintain that group counseling is not an economical use of the counselor's time. Even though it may provide the counselor with more "initial" counseling contacts, the group participants come to recognize the service provided by the group leader and successful group counseling experiences invariably lead to greater demands on the counselor's time by the individual participants following termination of the group.

There is no question in my mind concernng the element of efficient use of counselor time in utilizing group guidance with adolescents. However, I do question seriously the contention that group counseling does in fact provide a more efficient use of the counselor's time. I would suggest that each counselor would need to resolve this question in light of his own experiences.

ADVANTAGES OF THE GROUP

One of the basic reasons for forming the counseling group with adolescents is because of the tremendous strength of the peer group. The peer group can provide an experience unlike that of any other group, an experience that virtually all adolescents seek and need. Often an adolescent's acceptance by his peers in a counseling group will provide him with the support he needs to interact positively with his other peers outside the group setting.

The group counseling experience also provides the adolescent with opportunities to learn problem-solving techniques, develop social skills, and participate in decision making for himself and, to some extent, others in the group. All of these are skills which he will need to develop and refine if he is to function effectively as a member of the group as well as an individual in other relationships outside the group.

Within the group structure, some adolescents learn for the first time that they can *give* as well as receive help. This promotes a sense of usefulness within the adolescent in that he sees himself as a worthwhile and contributing person in the life of another person or persons. He sees that his comments and suggestions or support mean something to another person which in turn provides him with some additional insights into his own strengths and weaknesses. In essence, the group provides not only a structure in which one receives help, as in the traditional one-to-one counseling relationship, but also a structure in which one can contribute to the development of others.

Some students at this age find it easier to talk in a group of their peers than to an individual, even though that individual is a skilled and concerned counselor. Much of this attitude is a carryover from previous contacts with adults who are authority figures. In the group counseling session this adult figure tends to become just another member of the group and therefore less of a threat to the adolescent.

The astute counselor will recognize that some adolescents can benefit from the group counseling experience by simply being a member of the group. Although some adolescents are not especially verbal or contribute much to other members, they do learn and eventually resolve their own problems vicariously; i.e., by observing how other members in the group reslove their problems, the non-verbal adolescents will find solutions to their problems. The reverse is also true: the more verbal adolescents may come to realize that continuous verbalization within the group setting may not be the sole approach to resolving their concerns and that the role-model the nonverbal group member has established may be another way in which others find solutions to their problems.

Many adolescents, through real or imagined circumstances, have come to see the world as a rather cruel and uncaring place. Often the group counseling structure will provide them with opportunities to see that this concept may not be true in their relationships with all people and that the group can provide the support necessary to help the adolescents work through these feelings and attitudes.

FORMATION OF THE GROUP

There are any number of procedures used by the counselor to form the group. Some counselors simply inform the student that he has been selected to participate in a counseling group. Others, because of the feeling of pressure to see a number of students in a limited time period, attempt to "counsel" simultaneously with a group of students. (This notion of using group counseling as a means of saving time is a misunderstood notion held by many counselors and upon which I commented earlier.) Still others will invite students to participate in a counseling group after they have become relatively familiar with the student and his concerns. This procedure is by far the most realistic and professionally sound of all the above.

The invitation to join the group will be extended, or not, only after a personal interview with the prospective group member, with the emphasis in the interview being on what the student may gain through this kind of experience. The counselor explains the student's role, that of giving help to members in the group as well as receiving help from the group members and the counselor, should he decide to participate. Confidentiality with respect to the content of the group sessions should be stressed, and the prospective group member will need to commit himself to maintaining strict confidentiality for the duration of the group sessions as well as after the group has terminated.

The prospective group member should also be shown a list of the names of other students who are being considered for inclusion in the group and asked to indicate whether or not there is anyone on that list with whom he would not want to be placed in a group. Assuming there are none, and the student agrees to join the group, the counselor then considers the student a member of the group. If there were some students on the list whom the student would not like to have as a member of his group, the counselor would respect the wishes of the student and not include that person or persons in the group with that particular student.

Although the prospective member is given a list of names of others who are candidates for the group, the counselor must use some other guidelines in forming the group. He must be certain not to include in the same group first cousins, boy-girl friends, and siblings—unless these relationships are the reasons for forming the group; i.e., to work through sibling rivalry or boy-girl-friend relations.

The reasons for not including these students in the same group are readily apparent. In the case of the first cousins and siblings, it may tend to promote sibling rivalry, with the group counseling sessions being used as a public forum to air these concerns. Or siblings and/or first cousins may unite to form a block that has the effect of developing a group within the group, which tends to be counter-productive. Group members who are involved in boy-girl-friend relationships often have so much invested in each other emotionally that it is frequently difficult for either to deal objectively and independently with the concerns of the other members of the group. There is also the ever-present danger of losing one or both from the group as a result of the "breaking up" of the couple—which is more likely than not to happen in this age group. Therefore, if one is to attempt to provide stability in the group, one of the positive features of a counseling group, careful planning, which excludes these above-mentioned familial and personal relationships, will help to insure a successful beginning for the group counseling sessions.

By using this interview-invitation approach, the counselor has (1) made an assessment of the probable needs of the students who comprise the group, (2) assessed the probable contributions the student will make to the group, (3) set the parameters with respect to the personality composition of the group, (4) ascertained the probable extent to which each student would benefit from the group experience, and (5) establish in his mind the probable goals for the group.

Open and Closed Groups

Prior to forming the counseling group, the leader must determine whether the group will be an open group, wherein new members may come into the group when an opening occurs through the withdrawal of one of the members, or whether it will be a closed group, wherein all members will continue to participate in the group counseling sessions until termination of the group. The closed group will not accept new members should it be necessary for one or more of the original members to withdraw, whereas an open group invites another student to fill the vacancy created by the withdrawal of one of its members.

As in many of the other aspects of group counseling, there are advantages and disadvantages to each approach. Looking at the open group we find that by allowing new members to join from time to time throughout the duration of the group, the composition of the group is constantly changing. As new personalities come into the group, an entirely different set of dynamics comes into play, new or different ways of resolving problems may be introduced, and new problems may be brought to the group for resolution.

On the other side of the coin, time may be lost in "initiating" new members to the unique set of unwritten rules or understandings that each group sets as it develops; much old "material" may be rehashed from time to time to bring the new member(s) up to date; some group members may tend to see the new member(s) as an outsider and unconsciously attempt to keep him from becoming a fully functioning member of the group; and the counselor will need to go through the screening procedures as cited in "Forming the Group"— a time-consuming task in itself.

My preference with this age group is the closed group because the duration of the group is relatively short (8 to 16 weeks), maintenance of confidentiality is more easily managed, and adolescents seem to prefer that the membership of the group remains constant. Here is another instance in which one approach does not seem to hold a distinct advantage over the other. One needs to determine which will work better for his purposes, acknowledging the strengths and weaknesses of each. However, in this chaptper all examples and references will assume a closed group orientation.

Homogeneity Versus Heterogeneity in Group Composition

Another somewhat allied question that must be resolved before forming the group is that of homogeneity of group concern vs. heterogeneity of group concern. In other words, should the group be composed of adolescents with the same general concern such as a group of potential dropouts or should the group be composed of adolescents whose major concerns are essentially dissimilar? For example, the array of major concerns for each individual member could range from parental problems, to school failure, to getting along with one's peers, to deciding on the next step in a career decision, and so on.

Each approach has both advantages as well as disadvantages. The following lists will attempt to summarize some of the prominent advantages and disadvantages of each approach:

Homogeneous Group

Advantages:

Creates an attitude within the member that he does not "stand alone" with his problem;

Gives the individual an opportunity to learn new ways of approaching his problem by observing how others attack the same problem;

Facilitates the individual's discussion of the problem since he realizes that other members "know" what it is to have the problem;

Tends to promote acceptance of other members because of the individual's recognition that they are more nearly like him; and

Provides the leader initially with a singularly defined area of concern for all group members.

Disadvantages:

Increases the probability of collectivism; i.e., group members may tend to reinforce the negative aspects of their problems to the extent that it tends to debilitate rather than enhance the work of the group;

Increases the probability of the establishment of a substitute reality in which the group members "agree" to live with their problem rather than to continue to seek alternative solutions; and

Tends to reinforce the negative aspects of the problem to the extent that no "new" or creative solution to the problem is forthcoming.

Heterogeneous Group

Advantages:

Is a miniature representation of one's macrocommunity;

May create a feeling within the individual that his problem may be less serious and more manageable than some other person's problem in the group;

Provides the individual the opportunity to interact with others whose problems are different from his and to observe how he affects them; and

May provide certain individuals with the opportunity to "hide" within the group and yet receive help vicariously.

Disadvantages:

May spend too much of the group's time with too few of the member's concerns with the result being that some of the members may get very little support or help from the group;

Creates the possibility of the group "attacking" a given individual whose problem is too "different" or unacceptable to the majority of the other members; and

Taxes the skill and ability of the leader to interact effectively and equitably with each individual within the array of concerns presented.

In the final analysis the decision as to which kind of group to form comes down to three considerations: (1) the kind of problems to be dealt with; (2) the professional judgment of the counselor as to which approach would be best to use, knowing what he already knows about the prospective members; and (3) as often as not, the preference of the counselor.

Group Composition by Sex

There are two factors which must be taken into account when one deals with the sex composition of any counseling group of adolescents: The first is the social and emotional maturation of each prospective group member. This is a critical variable, and the counselor must have a good assessment of each prospective member so that he can determine the probable level of response of each to items that may be dealt with within the group counseling sessions. For example, a somewhat socially immature fourteen-year-old boy may not have the same social and emotional maturation of a fifteen-year-old girl and another seventeen-year-old boy who may be being considered for inclusion in the group.

The second factor to consider is the avowed purpose for meeting in the group. There would appear to be little reason to include girls in a counseling group of adolescent boys who are concerned about their feelings of homosexuality or including some boys in a counseling group formed to help a group of obese girls with their weight control.

Within the broad range of early and late adolescence there are some general guidelines that one should consider, beyond those two just mentioned, in forming groups for counseling. It is usually better to segregate by sex in the early adolescent range, regardless of the reason for forming the group. With the kinds of exceptions cited in the preceding paragraph, it is probably best to attempt to integrate the sexes for group counseling at the middle and upper levels of adolescence.

Early adolescents, particularly boys, tend to act out and/or reject members of the opposite sex during the counseling sessions. Therefore, if the counselor is constantly dealing with ways of maintaining order, there is little he can do to promote a good working relationship within the group. This can lead to the dissolution of the group because of the counselor's inability to maintain an atmosphere in which the counseling process can take place.

Older adolescents are at a point in their development in which they seek the approval and acceptance of members of the opposite sex. This attitude generally leads to a more nearly facilitative group experience, but it, too, can have a few drawbacks. Some adolescents will be so enamored by some members of the opposite sex that they spend much of their time performing for them rather than working on their concerns and those of other members of the group. Looking at these relationships from a positive point of view, we find that mixed sex groups in late adolescence permit group members to try out their sex roles, including learning ways to deal with members of the opposite sex in a rather secure and protected environment in which there exists a general feeling of positive regard between the sexes—a far superior setting than that in which many late adolescents learn their sex roles.

PHYSICAL SETTING

Privacy and comfort are the two primary physical prerequisites necessary for conducting group counseling. And of these two, privacy is paramount.

The usual setting provides comfortable, movable chairs that are generally placed in a circle with the counselor taking one of the seats as a member of the group. By placing the chairs in a circle each member, therefore, has a front seat and can see and hear and be seen and heard equally by every other member of the group.

An ideal setting would include a climate controlled environment, carpeted floors, adequate acoustics, comfortable chairs, adequate lighting, and again, complete privacy, free from any outside intrusion or interruption. This also means that the intercom system would not be operating in the room so its use would not interrupt the counseling session.

DURATION OF SESSIONS

There are some very practical considerations that contribute to the determination of the term or period of time which a counseling group will meet in a school setting. Traditionally, counseling groups are set around school calendars; i.e., they meet for a report card marking period (6-9 weeks), a half a semester (9 weeks), a semester (18 weeks), or an entire school year (approximately 36 weeks). Generally, however, counseling groups composed of adolescents find it somewhat difficult to span an extended vacation period without losing some continuity and are, therefore, generally scheduled to commence and/or terminate with natural breaks in the school calendar.

Obviously, there is no best schedule for any and all counseling groups of adolescents, and the final determination should be made by the counselor or arrived at jointly by the counselor and group members at the initial meeting of the group. By having the group members participate in this decision, the counselor assures that each individual is committed to meet with the group for the time period *they* set.

TIME AND FREQUENCY OF MEETINGS

As was the case in determining the duration of the life of the group, the daily school schedule will in great part determine the schedule of meetings of the group. Many school administrators will permit students to meet in group counseling sessions only during study periods, activity periods, or before or after the regular school day. This is a definite limitation on the flexibility of scheduling of the groups, but is generally adequate if the groups can be assured of that meeting time on a regularly scheduled basis.

Usually meetings are scheduled for once or twice a week for about 40 to 50 minutes, or the equivalent of a class period. Meeting times should be spaced far enough apart so that individual members will have time to reflect on the content of the group session, try out some of the ideas or skills learned in the group, and/or develop alternatives to problems and concerns presented by other members of the group.

A cardinal rule of meeting the counseling group schedule is that everything should be done to assure that the schedule of meetings will be maintained and that a group session will be cancelled only as the *last resort*. Students in this age group begin to invest of themselves in the group rather quickly and extensively. Consequently, a rather arbitrary cancellation of a group session can convey to the adolescent that the group counseling session is not as important as he has been led to believe, and, therefore, he becomes either disenchanted with the group, and especially the counselor, or he will not continue to commit himself to the group to the extent he once did. Inasmuch as the group should offer a sense of security and stability in the life of the adolescent, arbitrariness or indifference to the scheduling of group counseling sessions serves only to heighten the already tenuous feelings of insecurity and/or instability in many adolescents.

COUNSELOR'S ROLE

The role of the counselor is by responsibility and training different from and, at the same time, somewhat similar to the role of the student. The counselor has the responsibility for everything that transpires within the counseling session and to some extent for that which carries over into the counselee's life outside the group counseling session, as a result of his having participated and having gained direction from the group experience.

He must be sensitive to and prepared to act upon the feelings, ideas, emotions, and suggestions that emerge from the group. Not only must he have this sensitivity and preparation, he must also be aware of his own attitudes and emotions as he interacts with each member of the group as well as the group as a whole.

Without being judgmental, the counselor must be willing to let the group explore its feelings, attitudes, and ideas. He must also be accepting, but firm in his dealings with the group members.

Inasmuch as there are frequently some adolescents in a counseling group who are not always capable of defending themselves against verbal attacks from some of the other more outspoken members of the group, the counselor must be prepared to offer a degree of protection to them until such time as they learn to deal with the feelings of inadequacy they may have. In this capacity, the counselor will, in effect, be establishing a role model which he hopes the group members will emulate and internalize so that it will become a part of each counselee's way of dealing with other members of the group as well as carry over into their other day-to-day interactions. (Role modeling is not limited to the counselor's role in dealing with a counselee who is timid. This situation is used only as an example.)

The counselor is also responsible for the administrative and/or housekeeping chores of the group; e.g., providing adequate physical facilities; serving as a central clearinghouse for communications outside the group; and maintaining open communication between and among other interested school personnel. In terms of contemporary jargon, the counselor is responsible for facilitating the management and continued growth of all members of the group as well as all aspects of the group itself.

COUNSELEE'S ROLE

The primary role of the adolescent in the counseling group is to give help and support to others in the group who are seeking it and to utilize, to the extent possible, help from other group members. In conjunction with this role is an obligation that no member will attempt to "hurt" any other member of the counseling group.

Each group counseling member must be willing to listen to what each other member of the group is saying and *feeling*. A recognition of what the individual is experiencing at the feeling level must become part of each member's perception of every other member in the group. In essence, the counselee's role is an *active* rather than *passive* one. Other important aspects of the counselee's role are that of coming to the group session on time, being courteous, and maintaining confidentiality. Maintenance of these commitments will do much to assure the success of the group.

THE FIRST SESSION

The first session of the counseling group is unique with respect to every other session that follows. It is in this session that the ground rules are reviewed and the roles of the counselor and counselees are defined.

After all the participants have taken seats, the counselor introduces himself and reviews the ground rules that will be observed throughout the duration of the sessions. An important consideration is that the ground rules be kept to an *absolute minimum,* with the group being given the option of considering additional ground rules, should they feel the need at a later time.

The participants will be reminded that the ground rules were explained to each of them individually during their initial screening interview. However, since all members of the group are now present, they will all have an opportunity to hear them as a group and to ask questions or comment on them.

The ground rules consist of (1) maintaining strict confidentiality concerning everything that transpires within the group, (2) establishing a commitment to help each other, and (3) extending common courtesies to each other e.g., listening while others are speaking, getting to the sessions on time, and generally being considerate of the feelings of other members of the group. Adolescents have little difficulty in accepting these rules and will, on occasion, remind each other that they are being discourteous or that a certain comment is not really helpful.

The first session is characterized by participant anxiety and hesitancy, two understandable reactions. In order to help overcome these feelings and to set the tone for future sessions, I always introduce myself, using my title, and tell the group a little about myself and what they can expect from me as the counselor. It is important at this point not to inject a sense of artificiality into the group by dropping one's title. Mr. John Smith should introduce himself as Mr. Smith and not John Smith or John. This may seem like a moot point, but it must be remembered that on other occasions the counselor deals with these students with his title and to drop that title does create some rather awkward feelings within the adolescents. I have tried introducing myself both ways, with and without using my title, and when I used my first name only, the group members invariably referred to me only as "he" or "him" or "our counselor". But when I used my title, they, too, used it when addressing me or referring to me and were not placed in a position of trying to refer to me by my first name and still remain comfortable in doing so.

After I have introduced myself, I remind each member of the group that I did discuss with each of them individually some of the concerns that he had and that I am reasonably aware of why he is in the group and what he hopes to gain from being a group member. But since the individual member does not know why the other members are in the group, I ask each to give his first name, nickname, or name he would like to have us call him, tell why he chose to participate in the group, and what he hopes to gain from the experience. My approach is relatively non-directive in that I do not designate a sequence to follow in having the members introduce themselves. However, usually one student will begin and the sequence will follow from left or right of that person. But not always. Some adolescents are shy and will resist introducing themselves until all others have done so.

My role during the introductions is threefold: (1) to clarify and to reflect some of the feelings the students are expressing, (2) to help reduce some of the anxiety that is usually prevalent at this stage of the group's development, and (3) to serve as a role-model for all the group members. The last purpose is one of the primary functions of the counselor at this point. He must serve as a model that the group members will come to emulate in dealing with the verbal interactions that will transpire as the group meets over a period of time. Adolescents must be taught appropriate, helping responses in this setting; and rather than telling them what to say and how to say it, the counselor models this verbal and non-verbal behavior. Within a very short period of time—depending on the individuals within the group and the skill of the counselor—adolescents do begin to make feeling-level responses and do become co-counselors within the group.

As a result of the counselor's conscious efforts, modeling is also effective in the realm of non-verbal communication. Adolescents will exhibit attending behaviors of facing the group member speaking, maintaining comfortable eye contact, and leaning forward as a non-verbal gesture of support. To be sure, not all participants develop these behaviors to the same degree and some never develop them to any appreciable extent, but the vast majority do undergo some non-verbal behavioral changes.

After all members have introduced themselves, if necessary, I indicate that the group may talk about any of the concerns expressed by any of the members, a concern that was not expressed but could be introduced at this time, or any observation anyone would like to make concerning what they are currently feeling or thinking. One of three events then usually occurs: (1) someone will ask another individual some question concerning something he said when he was introducing myself; (2) someone will elaborate on what he said about himself; or (3) no one will say anything. If the last situation should occur, the best way to deal with the silence is to recognize it, pointing out to the group that sometimes it is a little difficult to get started in a new group like this and suggest that it might be beneficial to talk about these feelings of hesitancy or anxiety.

This invitation is usually enough to get the group started. However, if this does not initiate action, it is best not to try to force interaction by questioning the participants but rather to wait for voluntary response. It will come. It always does.

There are a few inherent dangers in the initial session of which the counselor must be aware. First, sometimes during the self-introductions a group member may be engaged in an extended discussion of his concern by one or more members of the group with the result that some of the other members may not get the opportunity to introduce themselves before the end of the session. This should be avoided. The primary purpose of the initial session is to introduce *every* member and his concern. Failure to do this may lead to a feeling of rejection by those who did not get to introduce themselves.

Second, it is often a difficult task, but every effort should be made to provide each member with an equal amount of time to contribute to the group during this first session. Some adolescents are particularly sensitive to other group members getting more than their "fair share" of the attention and will tend to reject the group and the counselor.

Finally, the counselor must guard against any group member telling "too much" about himself during this initial session. Unfortunately, some adolescents never get any attention unless it is through some kind of "captive audience" such as the group would be. In this situation, some will, for a variety of reasons—wanting to exhibit themselves, soliciting friendship, trying to meet their felt obligation to the group by making a contribution, responding to the anxiety produced by being in the group—tell more initially than they or the group can deal with adequately at that time. Therefore, it is the counselor's responsibility to protect these adolescents from themselves by responding to a *limited* amount of the material the adolescents are providing. The counselor does this by asking for clarification on some of the initial, less personal material; by trying to generalize the content to concerns of all group members; or by trying to turn the "floor" over to another group member to explore his concern.

Although I have cited this example from the first session, it can and does occur at any time throughout the duration of the group. The counselor must always be alert for this situation because the material is sometimes presented so rapidly or with so little indication that it is coming that it often becomes content for the group to deal with before the counselor can curtail it.

By cutting off this unrestrained input, the counselor allows the adolescent time to reflect on the material he is *ready* to share with the group at that time. This will help the adolescent avoid the very natural realization at a later time that he "told too much too soon." Also, the counselor will protect the group from having to deal with material that they, too, are not ready to deal with at this point in the development of the group.

As the time approaches for terminating the first group session, the counselor has several options open to him with respect to the technique or procedure he will use to end the session. Some counselors simply dismiss the group at some predetermined time or signal, such as a class bell. Others take it upon themselves as counselors to summarize for the group what they feel has transpired during that session. Others call upon one of the participants to summarize the session. Still others use a variety of these and other approaches from time to time.

In my groups, I always summarize the first session so that, again, I can model the technique, and, therefore, I do not put an undue demand on any one member of the group during this initial session. After the first session, however, I generally do ask a different member each time to summarize the session. On other occasions I may feel that a summary would not serve any useful purpose and may forego it.

As can be seen by just the few examples I have given here, the first session is crucial to the successful development of the counseling group. Although the group can be "lost" and need to be discontinued at any time, by recognizing and dealing effectively with these items in the beginning session, the counselor increases the probabilities of assuring a successful group counseling experience for the participants.

CONTINUATION OF GROUP SESSIONS

In terms of purpose, specific direction, and content, the first and last sessions are unique. This does not mean that the sessions between are shallow or bland. These are the sessions in which the adolescents will learn to deal more effectively with their concerns and problems while learning how to help others in the process.

Since time and space do not permit an in-depth analysis of what generally transpires in the group sessions between the first and last, I will point out only a few aspects with which the counselor must be prepared to deal. After the novelty of the group experience wears off, usually after the first several sessions, a certain amount of apathy tends to set in. This apathy may develop into some rather strong resistence if the counselor does not deal with it immediately. The best way to accomplish this is to bring it to the attention of the group so they, too, are aware of what the group is experiencing. The counselor must help them determine why they have fixated at this level of the group's development and help them over this non-productive stage.

Another common occurrence that the counselor must be prepared to handle is that of the adolescent who, feeling secure in the group, begins to act out. Acting-out adolescents often tax the upper limits of the skill of the counselor. Again, one of the better ways of dealing with such behavior is to help the individual and the group recognize it and explore its causes, as well as possible ways of dealing with it within the group.

Formation of cliques or sub-groups within the group is a natural phenomenon with all age groups, but is particularly strong in early adolescence. At this age, boys and girls are looking to develop closer personal ties with one or two other members of the same sex. Later adolescence is characterized by a search for a closer relationship with members of the opposite sex and could lead to a sexual pairing in which one member of one sex will support and defend almost blindly the point of view of a selected member of the opposite sex.

Since the group is a micro-representation of the participants' macro-community, the counselor is afforded an excellent opportunity to deal with cliques, boy-girl relations, and sub-groups in a larger society as part of the group's work. In essence, the group with those inherent relationships becomes a good laboratory setting in which the participants can explore and resolve for their own purposes these in-group relationships.

The group also goes through some rather definite developmental stages as the participants meet over a period of time. In other words, the group itself has a life cycle that can be recognized and used by the counselor to the advantage of the individual participants.

It is not the purpose of this chapter to deal with this process in any depth. However, Bonney, in Gazda, (1969) provides an excellent account of this process.

Finally, the counselor must keep in mind the fact that all of the group sessions will not go smoothly. There will be times when he will need to call upon all his skills and insights in order simply to maintain the group as a cohesive unit. On other occasions, he will need to guard against group euphoria which may result from a relatively meaningful group session for the majority of members. Only the most skillful and facilitating of group counselors will be able to sustain a fully functioning counseling group for the duration of the life of the group.

PRECAUTIONARY MEASURES

On the whole, the ground rule which must constantly be reinforced is the one dealing with confidentiality. It is often difficult for adolescents to maintain confidentiality when other classmates, friends, and even teachers often inquire as to what transpires in the group counseling sessions. Peers who are non-group members often exert much pressure on participants to tell them what was discussed in the group. More often than not this is a mater of idle curiosity. But when the non-group member is told that the content of the group sessions is confidential, this can be taken as a challenge to find out more, or it can create antagonism between the adolescent making the inquiry and the group member.

One way of handling this before it develops as a problem for any of the group members is to tell them that other students and friends will, because of natural curiosity, ask them what they are doing in the group sessions. An honest answer would be to tell them that the group discusses subjects such as school, studying, getting along with others, and other similar topics. This answer is usually enough to satisfy the majority of information seekers. Essentially, what the counselor tries to convey to the group members is the idea of not making the commitment to confidentiality appear to be a secret conspiracy or have the group itself appear to be a privileged group.

Another group of people with whom the adolescent group member must deal in terms of his commitment to confidentiality is the voyeuristic teacher. Some teachers become quite threatened by this group of adolescents meeting to discuss with the teachers' peer—the counselor—anything they want to discuss—*even* the teachers themselves. Fortunately, the number of overt, voyeuristic teachers is relatively small on any given faculty. However, they remain a group that can bring much pressure to bear on adolescents to share with them the content of the group meetings, particularly anything that might have some real or *imagined* bearing on the teachers themselves.

This is another potential problem that can be averted by some good public relations on the part of the counselor. For the counselor establishing groups for the first time in a given school, a brief announcement at a faculty meeting explaining the purposes, functions, advantages, and limitations of group counseling will generally satisfy the vast majority of faculty members. Special emphasis should be placed on the counselor's role, pointing out that whatever transpires in the group is confidential, underscoring that any reference to teachers will remain within the group. It is also helpful to point out that the group counseling sessions are not designed to be gripe sessions about teachers or the school, although traditionally this is where some of the early sessions begin, but that group counseling will serve as a vehicle through which these adolescents will begin to look at themselves more objectively.

This is also a good opportunity to let the teachers know that as a result of the group sessions adolescents often find courage to come to teachers to discuss problems with them and that the teachers would be of additional help if they were receptive to them. Generally, teachers are quite willing to assume this role and cooperation is **virtually unanimous.**

Along the same lines, that of communicating the program of group counseling to other interested persons, is the question of requesting written permission from the parents of potential group members for their children to participate in the group. Although at first brush this suggestion may seem to have some merit, further reflection tends to underscore its weaknesses.

The request for written permission tends to raise suspicion in the minds of parents concerning the *real* purpose of the group; i.e., what is this really all about? What is wrong with my child that he needs this special treatment? Why are "they" interested in having my child tell all his problems to a group of his friends and a stranger (the counselor)? The list of suspicions raised are probably limited only by the creative imaginations of the individual parents.

Requiring written parental permission for adolescents to participate in group counseling sessions does not appear to me to be defensible on any grounds. If, being a professional counselor, one engages in counseling adolescents on a one-to-one basis and since the principles remain the same, a counselor should not seek written parental permission to function with a group of adolescents in a counseling session. What makes the group setting so unique that parental permission must be granted in order for an adolescent to participate in the process? Many unnecessary anxieties may be created within the adolescents concerning what might happen to them in the group because parental permission is necessary in order to participate. In summary, unless there is a school ruling that requires written parental permission for *all* forms of counseling, to seek it for participation in group counseling is unnecessary, and, I submit, counterproductive for the purposes of group counseling.

There may be one other issue with which the counselor may need to deal as the group begins to meet on its regular schedule, and that relates to persons outside the group who may raise questions concerning the techniques or methods that the counselor may be employing within the group. With the recent development of the Human Potential Movement and the multifarious "techniques" that have evolved, it has become necessary, unfortunately, to ask questions of some group counselors with respect to the techniques they are employing during their group sessions.

In my opinion, in this setting and under these conditions, the only acceptable general technique to employ with adolescents in group counseling is verbal. Because of time limits, age of the members, and level of experience and skill of the average counselor, non-verbal or tactile techniques are unacceptable and potentially dangerous, not only to the adolescent participants but also to the total counseling program as well.

Therefore, extreme care should be taken to utilize only verbal techniques, such as role playing, simulation, and group discussions, with which the counselor is familiar and competent. Under *no* circumstances should the counselor hesitate to clarify this point with anyone who should inquire, and he would do well to stress this point when informing the faculty about the group counseling program.

FINAL SESSION

As was stated earlier, the final group session, like the initial group session, is unique in its purposes and content. This is the session in which the participants come face-to-face with the realization that the group as they have come to know it will cease to exist.

For some adolescents this is very difficult to accept, while others take it in stride and accept it as a matter of course. In order to avert any possible "separation anxiety", the counselor needs to prepare the members of the group for the eventual termination of the group counseling sessions. This is best accomplished by having the group recognize several meetings prior to termination that the date of termination of the group is imminent.

It is at this point in the group's development that a gradual weaning process is introduced. The process is designed to have the counselee move from the status of a group member who is sensitized to the support of the group to an individual who for the most part can make decisions and deal with his problems and concerns from an internal frame of reference. A counselor cannot hope to help the individual attain this level of functioning by simply telling him at the beginning of the final session that this is the last session and that it is hoped he has gained much from the experience. This realization may come as too great a shock for some adolescents who have become quite personally committed to the group.

The recognition that the group will soon terminate often prompts additional input from those adolescents who feel that if they are going to receive help from the group they should seek it now. This affects the group and the participants in two ways: (1) the group has much additional material with which to deal in a relatively short time period, and (2) some of the participants become less actively involved because they begin to curtail their personal commitment to the group.

Under this set of circumstances, the counselor often finds himself in the somewhat awkward position of trying to have the group maintain a high level of effective functioning while simultaneously preparing the group for termination. This is another example in which the best way to handle the situation is for the counselor to help the group recognize the dynamics of the situation and to deal with it as best they can. Once the adolescent begins to recognize what is happening in the group at this point in time as well as his role in it, he can begin to deal with it more effectively.

In some counseling groups, there may be adolescents who begin to show signs of resisting the upcoming termination because of a dependency need they have developed for the group. It is important that the counselor help these adolescents understand what they are experiencing through acknowledging that this sometimes occurs in group work, and then set out to provide them with the support in the group necessary to overcome this dependence need.

During the final session, all the group members should be told that they may come to the counselor any time in the future for individual counseling, or if they feel that they would like to participate in another counseling group to let the counselor know so that he may consider the counselees' requests. Although the question of additional counseling following the termination of the group may be raised by a group member very early in the life of the group, this invitation should not be extended or volunteered by the counselor until at least the next to last or preferably the last group counseling session. If the invitation is extended too early, some of the group members may become less involved, relatively speaking, waiting for the group to terminate so they can seek individual counseling.

This attitude in and of itself is not bad, but it does set the stage for a type of group drainage. Contributions individuals might make to the group in terms of sharing their concerns, with the expectation of having the group help find solutions, will never become part of the group content; therefore, the group will not have had the opportunity to experience and "know" the concerns and feelings of these individauls.

One technique that is helpful to both the counselees and the counselor in starting the last session is to have each group member, including the counselor, tell what he feels he has gained from the group counseling experience. This also serves to help summarize the work of the group and to tie up any loose ends.

Another technique is to have each member write a summary of his feelings concerning the group experience and bring it with him to the last meeting of the group, knowing that the summary will be read to the group by another member. The summary may be anonymous or it may be signed by the group member. These summaries always generate group discussion and serve to help the group members terminate the group more easily.

Whatever technique the counselor chooses to employ in terminating the group, he must be guided by the principle of independence; i.e., in the future the counselees will no longer have the support and help of the group in reaching decisions or seeking alternatives to their concerns. If this can be accomplished, the counselor can feel reasonably certain that he has met his obligation to the members of the group with respect to developing independence of the group.

SUMMARY

Group counseling is an approach other than the traditional one-to-one counseling relationship that can be employed effectively in working with adolescents in the school setting. Not to be confused with group guidance, group counseling is a technique utilized with a relatively small number of normal adolescents (6-10), over a set period of time, with the emphasis on individual growth and development resulting from the group experience.

The origins of group counseling are somewhat obscure. Guidance information sessions, case conferences, group dynamics, and the child study approach have all contributed to the technique we now recognize as group counseling.

In order for any counseling group to be successful, many factors must be taken into account. These include the primary purposes of the group, formation of the group, open and closed groups, homogeneity versus heterogeneity in group composition, group composition by sex, physical setting, duration of sessions, time and frequency of meetings, the counselor's role, and the counselee's role. Factors which need to be given optimum attention are the first session, continuation of group sessions, precautionary measures, and the final session. Possessing the necessary skills and being aware of all of these factors and the importance of each, the counselor can conduct counseling groups successfully.

REFERENCES

Bennett, M.: *Guidance and Counseling in Groups,* 2nd ed. New York, McGraw-Hill, 1963.

Bonney, W. B.: in Gazda, G. M. (Ed.) *Theories and Methods of Group Counseling in Schools.* Springfield, Thomas, 1969.

Gazda, G. M.: *Basic Approaches to Group Psychotherapy and Group Counseling.* Springfield, Thomas, 1968.

Gazda, G. M.: *Group Counseling: A Developmental Approach.* Boston, Allyn and Bacon, 1971.

Glanz, E. C., and Hayes, R. W.: *Groups in Guidance* 2nd ed. Boston, Allyn and Bacon, 1967.

Glass, S. D.: *The Practical Handbook of Group Counseling.* Baltimore, B.C.S. Publishing Co., 1971.

Kemp, C. G.: *Foundations of Group Counseling.* New York, McGraw-Hill, 1970.

Lifton, W.: *Working with Groups* 2nd ed. New York, Willey and Sons, 1966.

Mahler, C. A.: *Group Counseling in the Schools.* Boston, Houghton-Mifflin, 1961.

Ohlson, M. M.: *Group Counseling.* New York, Holt, Rinehart, and Winston, 1970.

Thelen, H.: *Dynamics of Groups at Work.* Chicago, University of Chicago Press, 1954.

CHAPTER II

GROUP COUNSELING
OF THE DISADVANTAGED

THOMAS K. ALLAN AND KATHRYN H. ALLAN

Why Groups for the Disadvantaged?	Selecting Group Members
Who Are the Disadvantaged?	Techniques
	Change in the Individual
	Conclusion
	Selected Readings

TYPES OF PROBLEM-intervention offered in our culture for dealing with the disadvantaged include crisis-counseling, preventive education, institutionalization, and subsidization (e.g., welfare).
Both institutionalization and subsidization are being criticized from
both philosophic and economic points of view. Preventive education
is certainly a respectable means for dealing with future problems.
However, there are no immediate rewards, and there are not enough
behavior-modifiers to do both preventive education and the sort of
crisis-intervention counseling that is more prevalent now. Current
ethics—admittedly questionable—do not permit us to sacrifice our
clients in crisis while we use our energies in developing a preventive
program. Thus, counseling in our culture typically is of a crisis-intervention style.

This style can nevertheless act to retrain the client to new ways of
problem-solving; the line between education and counseling is a thin
one. Counseling is a goal-oriented education, tailor-made to individuals or small groups, and is, therefore, particularly effective for
people whose cultural and financial disadvantages inhibit their profit-
ing from traditional mass-education opportunities.

WHY GROUPS FOR THE DISADVANTAGED?

Why is group counseling the preferred method of treatment for the disadvantaged? Obviously, the opportunity exists for this method to be more efficient than individual counseling; more clients can be helped by a single counselor. This opportunity is especially poignant in the ghetto, where there are fewer counselors available and less money. Furthermore, personal problems are more acute, with frequent financial crises, greater mental and physical illness, crowdedness, underemployment, and undereducation.

More and more counselors, including leaders in the field, are becoming personally convinced of the particular effectiveness of the group approach. There are several reasons cited for using groups to elicit behavior change. The group serves as a laboratory for trying out new behaviors without great personal risk. There are more models—the other group members—from whom to learn. The similarity between real life and the group setting, as opposed to individual therapy, leads to a rapid transfer of group learning to outside problems. Because all members have an opportunity to participate in the helping role, the disadvantaged individual has the chance to gain self-confidence and see himself as a winner. The phenomenon of group cohesiveness allows group approval to act as a much stronger reinforcer of behavioral change than most individual therapists can provide.

WHO ARE THE DISADVANTAGED?

This chapter began as a collection of kernels of wisdom about what might be useful techniques for group-counseling of the poor. These kernels mostly were born in group-counseling experiences of other types of "disadvantaged"—drug addicts, school dropouts and women, for example. However, there is really no reason not to be straight with the reader and encourage him to think, as we do, of all persons with troubles as being disadvantaged. We have found that the counseling techniques that succeed will succeed regardless of the stated problem (although there are minor refinements for different stated problems).

A disadvantaged person can be defined more narrowly as anyone whose life-style is divergent from that of the American middle-class male. Such persons usually include the poor, the ill, the elderly, many ethnic minority groups, women, drug addicts and alcoholics, prisoners, school dropouts, hippies, and unmarried pregnant teenagers. The disadvantaged who can be helped are fewer; however, the type of group counseling most available in our institutions professes a broad type of middle-class value system which must be accepted by the client as a goal if he is to be aided by the counselor. There *are* other types of groups, but they are usually not available to the above disadvantaged, especially the poor, because these groups are not subsidized by society. Thus, we are faced with the irony of the "not middle class" being permitted to join only middle-class groups. The exclusion is not only caused by lack of money, it should be noted, but by lack of access of other types—such as knowledge of availability.

SELECTING GROUP MEMBERS

Thus, here we will deal only with those disadvantaged who can be helped by the subsidized or volunteer groups most likely to be available to them. "Being helped" is defined as achieving a greater number of personal goals within the existing middle-class system. This is a practical choice, since any other definition of help is ultimately likely to elicit censure from this society, and group definition of help in other ways must either cease to exist or go underground. Another advantage of this choice is the fact that group-learned behaviors are more likely to be reinforced in the societal environment.

Successful counselors, just as successful clients, plan progress toward their goals in "doable bits." If counselors are not successful, they will likely become discouraged, or society will no longer reward them. In keeping with this assumption, the selection of clients with whom to work first becomes critical.

We advocate selecting clients who are likely to make the greatest gain with a minimum of therapeutic input, thereby encouraging continued societal and therapeutic support. The best advertisement for any type of counseling is a client who is happy with his movement toward his goals and who communicates this fact in word and behavior.

Selection should take into account the personal motivation of its group member; after initial exposure to the group experience, he should wish to make a commitment to the group that he will work on his problems in the group. This is a principle of such groups as

Odyssey, a drug addiction group which requires a promise of 30-day residence including abstinence from drugs as a sign of commitment. Transactional analysts often ask in the first session if the client will work for a cure (as opposed to playing games).

Such commitment is evidence to the therapist that the particular client has some confidence in the group process and intends to work within it. Social welfare agencies sometimes "pay" their clients to get help, by withholding monetary assistance for non-compliance; or, alternatively, offering extra rewards for compliance. One government agency, in an experiment with underemployed men, paid them for each group attendance. This worked badly, because the men were absent whenever a better-paying task was available. Furthermore, those who did come did not feel obligated to participate; they had done their job by merely showing up.

Some counselors like to work with clients who "can only go up," in other words, who are in such bad shape and need such a lot of help that (it appears) anything the counselor does will be useful. Thus, the counselor predicts he will be successful with ease and the client also will benefit.

We do not recommend this selection route. For one thing, the most unhappy of the disadvantaged are likely to have among their difficulties such needs as food and adequate housing—items which the therapist cannot provide, but which, at the same time, are more primary than the client's psychological health. It is difficult to worry about one's ability to communicate meaningfully when one is hungry.

Often a group can alleviate the problems peculiar to this type of client by acting as an information and referral system, especially if some of the others have had similar experiences.

To insure success and (part of the definition of success) continuation of the group, the best clients are those who not only have already made some commitment to group participation but who have, on balance, the most to gain *and* the least to lose. Among the disadvantaged, examples of poor-risk members include those who have had some status among their peers which is based on peer-group loyalty. An example of this is one group which was started by some white middle-class urban planners concerned about lack of communication between black and white community leaders regarding the city's housing problems. A black militant, though initially pleased with the opportunity for a confrontation with the white power-holders, soon reported censure from his constituency. They said he was seen as "making deals with the establishment". He began to worry about losing his position in the community.

Another member of this same group was an elected politician who was afraid if he stayed in the group he would change his behavior. This, he predicted, would cause his constituents to doubt his decisions. He had his whole career to lose.

Another loss which might be major for some would be giving up a familiar, albeit unpleasant, life contract. For example, some clients habitually externalize the locus of responsibility for their state of well-being. The fact that racism exists in employment opportunity serves as an excuse for some to remain unemployed and causes certain minority group members to despair rather than to follow the example of other, more self-determined, members of their subgroup. There is a small coal-mining town in Pennsylvania which is half populated with men unemployed for twenty years, since the mine closed. These men refuse to move because, they claim, should the mines reopen, they would lose their job seniority. For one of these men to participate successfully in a group trying to help him improve his life, he would have to admit he had wasted twenty years—a difficult act.

A person who has staked all of his confidence in a single, rigid behavioral strategy for coping with fears of failure stands to lose from joining a group. A woman with a domestic job which she disliked and which paid badly, believed strongly that she could improve her job status if she only knew how to type. For years, she said she didn't have time at present to work toward her goal. As might be expected, the group urged her to take the time, in spite of the possible loss, for her, of either failing the course, or passing it only to discover that learning to type doesn't guarantee a secretarial job. It is understandable that she was not willing to test the reality of a dream which pleasantly occupied much of her time.

As mentioned, the authors led a group in a southern city which aimed at increasing communication and cooperation between the city's black and white leaders. They decided to test the assumption that greater loss than gain for an individual would mean lack of optimal participation. It was found that the half of the group with the most to lose (by the leaders' estimates) attended less than half as many group meetings as the members with less to lose. An example of the latter was a retired banker/former mayor. He was no longer running for office and was rich enough to care little about making his business more successful. By virtue of his age and past accomplishments he was so thoroughly established in the community that he tended to establish community norms. He attended every meeting. An example of a man with a great deal to lose was the white politician mentioned above who felt his entire career could be affected adversely by the group. He soon dropped out.

Another criterion for selecting clients for maximum group success is that of choosing persons whose divergence from the middle class is one of knowledge and skills, rather than of values or goals. Values and goals take longer to change and are less amenable to manipulation. They are usually a complex rationalization of behavior and giving them up would be incongruent with innumerable previous actions. Working directly on behavior change through acquisition of new information and skills permits the client to alter his values gradually, with no loss of self-respect.

A state employment service had as its policy to "salt" its groups of unemployed disadvantaged with a few persons who had successfully retained jobs for some time. Job retention skills were taught without ever directly attacking the inappropriate goal of the unemployed men, which was a day's work without thought to the future.

This brings up another selection problem concerning the composition of the group. A group should be heterogeneous in regard to the particular variable that the leader is attempting to modify, as in the above example, where persons with varying degrees of competency in the skill to be acquired are placed among those with relatively low competency. This is often done with the academically troubled, where some persons are available who have already been successful with new study skills and are combined with those who have had no experience with them. Ex-drug addicts and ex-alcoholics are much more successful at influencing the behavior of fellow addicts than are doctors or social workers without direct experience. It is felt that this phenomenon may be related to the "credibility factor", which requires that a person must believe he can change before he can actually progress, and this belief is facilitated by identification with persons who are similar to himself.

TECHNIQUES

Is is not our intention to limit ourselves to a single theoretical approach or technique. Our observation is that theorists from vastly different theoretical backgrounds end up agreeing on the same techniques of behavior change. Our own eclectic approach draws on many theories, but a rational-behavioral framework guides us. This is apparently particularly useful for middle-class counselors who are working with the disadvantaged. It is difficult but necessary for the client to have feelings of trust in the therapist; this is more readily accomplished when the motivation for counselor behavior is most obvious to the client and gets results early.

The rational approach focuses on the client's expectations, what he is doing to reach his goals, and how his expectations and beliefs about reality are influencing his behavior. In our culture, people have come to believe in irrational concepts which do not help them to reach their goals and often have deleterious effects on their success. An example of an irrational belief is that a person should be thoroughly competent, adequate, and achieving if he is to consider himself worthwhile. A way this is often expressed is, "Anything worth doing is worth doing well". This idea leads to avoidant behavior when a person experiences failure early in the learning cycle.

For instance, school becomes a place to avoid for many disadvantaged persons because of their poor performance in the past. A truly rational person learns all he can under present circumstances and works on improving his coping with the problem; he does not give up in the face of short-term failure. An advantage of the rational philosophy is that it can be taught in groups by rewarding approximations of the desired behavior. Many schools now grade student progress as complete or incomplete rather than Pass-Fail, in an attempt to reward growth, no matter how slow.

CHANGE IN THE INDIVIDUAL

The Placebo Factor

We are going to consider five components of change in the individual. The first is the placebo, or credibility factor; this is the belief that group members have that the group leader, the other members, and the group activities can change him. This belief depends upon such variables as counselor reputation, the client's belief in the group process, social status of the group activity, the client's ability to identify with other group members, apparent validity of the group activities with regard to changing people, and the "new-experience" factor, which serves in the initial stages to hold the client's attention.

The leader's role in maintaining the placebo factor is to model constructive credibility in a genuine, non-cynical way that serves to reinforce similar confidence in the group process on the part of the client. One way of doing this would be for the leader to engage in self-disclosures which tell how this and other groups have helped him.

Defining Belief Systems

Another component of change is the client's ability to define his belief system. The belief system is how the person construes events. An important element of definition is accurate communication. Because of the many listeners and interpreters available, a group serves a particularly useful function in giving feedback to clear up miscommunication. A client who continually used phrases such as "that's life", "it's God's will", and "you can't fight it", was told by a group member: "You don't want to take any responsibility for your own life". This clarification of the client's original statements permitted him to become aware of one of his basic assumptions about life.

The group can often detect inconsistencies between a member's professed values and those values which actually guide his day-to-day behavior. One member in a group of disadvantaged persons evidenced lack of concern about working to improve her life conditions out of a martyr-like belief that her self-sacrificing acts would ultimately be rewarded. When confronted with the fact that there was no proof that increasing her present happiness would cause later deprivation, she became less self-denying.

In the above example, the original belief system was something related to, "I'll get pie in the sky when I die, if I suffer now". Yet the person professed not to believe in heaven. The group's aid in pointing out that her two beliefs were mutually exclusive helped her to work more efficiently toward solving her problems. The leader can often help by clarifying to a member what other members are telling him.

Client Defensiveness

We want to examine the passive as opposed to the aggressive/ directive approach to dealing with defensiveness. A popular method of dealing with client defensiveness is one usually associated with Carl Rogers. This includes acceptance, reflection of the client's feelings, and clarification of client communications. Of these, acceptance is probably the most powerful, in that like some oriental methods of fighting, the client defeats his own defensiveness in the absence of aggressive force. There is also a tendency for persons to take the side of the argument left untaken. Arguing with a defensive client can increase his defensiveness. The group might operate more effectively by exhibiting a Rogerian stance.

In a group composed of young people with drug problems, many members argued vociferously for legalization of all drugs. Rather than countering this argument, the leader accepted the member's arguments to the point where several persons began to state the deleterious effects that the use of drugs had had on their schoolwork. When the client is not forced to expend his energies to defend a current belief system, he has an opportunity to use those energies in examining alternative views.

Applying this concept to the rational/ directive approach in counseling, the leader may begin by accepting the group member's goals and trying to get him to expand them and refine his methods for achieving them. He should not begin with criticism or he will turn the client off before he starts.

The first step is to get the client to set some goals. The leader accepts them. If goals are vague and ambiguous, he helps to clarify them. He helps the member to break the goals down into immediate objectives.

As the client gains confidence and trust in the leader and group members, they may shift to a more confronting mode of dealing with defensiveness. One belief that clients defend most ardently is the idea that they *are* their behavior. The leader and group can attack this belief by pointing out that "worthwhile persons can indulge in non-worthwhile behavior". They can ask the member if he knows a person he believes to be intelligent who has poor academic achievement. This strategy can be generalized to other areas.

In this area of discussion of defensiveness, it has been the authors' observation that in groups whose leaders behave as participant leaders, defensiveness is less. We theorize that when leaders model openness and risk-taking in the attempt to reconstrue their own belief systems, the group follows their example.

Challenging the Belief System

All of the steps in the change process—credibility, defining the belief system, defending the belief system—are merely precursors to this next step. Unless the clients arrive at a point where they begin to question their previous modes of construing their environments, no real change in behaviors is likely to occur. Dollard and Miller, Ellis, and Kelly have theorized, and we believe, that human behavior flows from the internalized sentences people tend to repeat to themselves.

Active leader behavior, passive leader behavior, and experiential activity of group members all seem to effect changes in their internal sentences. Three types of active leader behavior are modeling, lecturing, and selective reinforcement. As mentioned above, with highly defensive persons, modeling is more likely than lecturing to lead to successful problem-solving. However, when clients are highly motivated to change their behavior, and lack of information is the major source of trouble, lecturing can be an extremely efficient means of modification. Other group members can participate in both activities. It should be noted that in the case of groups where the leader is not from a disadvantaged background, it is less likely that he can serve as a believable model. Referring back to the example given in the section on selection, it was found that in the employment service group, successful, employed disadvantaged persons could most effectively model appropriate behaviors for those as yet unemployed.

Lecturing by the employment service counselors, who came from the middle and upper middle class, proved relatively unsuccessful in this type of group.

A group of underemployed fathers attended an informal lecture on birth-control methods, given by the leader. Afterwards they were encouraged to ask questions and discuss different methods. Members were highly enthusiastic about the lecture period; furthermore, most went on to try some of the methods. It is obvious that basic information was vital to attaining the goals of these men. It should be pointed out, however, that clarification (the discussion) is important.

In selective reinforcement, the group leader not only contributes to reinforcing certain behaviors but also encourages other group members to work upon the target member or problem. Contingencies can be positive or negative, although it may be difficult to determine which is a reinforcer for a particular client. Women in a career counseling group (disadvantaged, by our original definition) reinforced each other for increasing their economic valuations of their labor within the household. Out of this change a new self-concept and confidence emerged. Several of the women decided to market their previously unrealized skills.

The passive approach to inducing self-challenge is that of unconditional positive regard—providing a climate of acceptance wherein a client can devote his energies to exploring changes in values rather than defending the old. In groups where the leader is white and most of the members are black, the hostility felt by the black members tends to be dissipated in the presence of an empathic, understanding acceptance.

One of the most effective methods of getting at "gut-level" belief systems is role-playing. The client can play his expressed self, his hidden self, or the self of significant others in his environment as he perceives them. New perceptions emerge as the group member experiences his feelings in each assigned role. A practical example of the use of this technique occurred in an employment service training group, where the members were encouraged to alternately play the roles of job interviewer, interviewee, and future employer. Through this experience, a greater understanding emerged as to why each person behaved in the manner in which he did. Group members were able to see why job interviewers felt pressure to screen out applicants who appeared to be poor employment risks, e.g., had poor appearance, lack of motivation, poor communication skills. When the client played himself, he became aware of and verbalized his own lack of skills in handling job interviews and engaging in job-retaining behaviors. In the role of employer, he realized the conflict between profit and humanitarian motives.

Planning Change Strategies

It is the feeling of the authors that the part of therapy that is most demanding of the therapist's skills is the planning of change strategies.

It is our feeling that this must be done in a "homework" style, in "doable bits", which, however, are sufficiently challenging to capture the client's imagination. At the beginning of a group, most of this planning will be done by the therapist, but other group members will quickly catch on by virtue of experiencing what has worked for them and may eventually become more adept than the therapist at making such assignments.

The expression "homework" refers to tasks suggested to the group member to perform outside the group environment, about which activities he will be expected to report to the group, often a powerful reinforcer. "Doable bits" refers to the idea that many clients have engaged in self-defeating, overly high, self-expectation. A "doable bit" is something that the client can reasonably accomplish but is not so insignificant that he doesn't feel challenged by attempting it. Logically, the client must learn to crawl before he walks. Of course, assignments should be relevant to the client's goals.

An example of the above is that of a group member who was having difficulty getting dates. He rarely asked a girl out and each defeat required a month of recovery before he would try again. Instead of asking him to "try to get a date with a girl", the therapist suggested homework for this client of obtaining five legitimate refusals of dates. By "legitimate" it was meant that he would not purposely try to be refused, but would instead use his usual manner of asking for dates.

In this particular case, he did not completely succeed at his assignment in that he only obtained three rejections. He gave up out of sheer frustration. The group complimented him on the fact that he had accomplished 60 percent of his assignment. The group asked him how he felt about the refusals; he said he didn't feel too badly, since getting refused had been his goal. The group questioned him as to how he had managed to succeed in his homework. He reported on the various ways (although he was unaware of their inappropriateness) that he had used to approach each girl. These means were discussed in the group. New strategies for approaching girls were suggested by the leader and the group members. The member's assignment for the following week was to get an acceptance of a date. This case is an illustration of the problem where success is prevented by the inability to deal with failure. When the client realized that failures are merely inconvenient, at worst, and learning experiences, at best, his attitude toward risk-taking changed in a more positive direction.

Many or most self-defeating group members have set for themselves goals that are inappropriately high. The client learns that every expectation that he has is doomed to failure. In order to reverse this self-defeating philosophy, the leader and members teach each other to plan for themselves hurdles whose chances of being overcome are quite high. Soon, the client learns to expect success instead of failure. It appears to the authors that this change in expectation, along with increased skill in setting appropriate goals, results in great changes in self-concept. The authors are not certain why people tend to set overly-high goals; it may be parental training, it may be a need to compensate for past failures, or, more likely, it may be a defense in that if one sets extremely high goals, he can console himself when failure results with the thought that practically no one could have been able to accomplish what he has selected to do. The satisfaction that accrues from accomplishing doable bits is often great enough to convince the client to give up his old self-defeating behaviors. Ultimately he may, in doable steps, reach the higher goal he set for himself, and thus eat his cake and have it, too.

It should be noted that in the above example, the group reinforced a client who had achieved only 60 percent of his assigned homework. A term for this is "rewarding successive approximations of behavior". Too often, a person is punished unless an entire task is completed; he then is discouraged from working at all toward the goal. Encouragement for behavior which becomes closer and closer to appropriate keeps the group member moving in the desired direction and learning continues.

Occasionally, the anxiety which prevents the client from engaging in homework assignments is so great that it defeats the accomplishment of the task. The most poignant case in the authors' experience was a forty-five year old man who for the past many years had not been able to maintain an erection long enough to have intercourse. He could become aroused, but immediately after penetration he lost his erection. The homework assignment given him was one suggested by Frankl's theory of *paradoxical intention*. That is, he was instructed that, upon penetration, he was to attempt to lose his erection as quickly as possible. The theory behind this assignment was that his fear of loss of erection was causing his problem. The client was intrigued by this assignment. He tried it twice with his girlfriend and each time he successfully accomplished the assignment—that is, he lost his erection. On the third attempt, as the result of a minor quarrel preceding the lovemaking, he was particularly enthusiastic about the assignment; he genuinely did not mind losing his erection. Under these circumstances, his anxiety was greatly reduced, and the natural stimuli of the situation caused him to maintain an erection to orgasm, his first in twenty-five years! His report to the group was ecstatic. Although from time to time he continued to have anxiety difficulties, the problem continued to diminish.

The authors realize that the previous example does not apply necessarily to the disadvantaged; it was presented for its dramatism and clarity. The implications of this technique could well be applied to disadvantaged persons who are so anxiety-bound during job interviews that they do not function optimally. They become so tongue-tied out of fear of not obtaining the position that they are unable to communicate their skills to the prospective employer. Here, the assignment would be to "care less" about making a proper impression. The applicant would be instructed to think of the employer as a peer and to think of reasons why the job may not be particularly desirable. This technique often results in a loss of self-consciousness which impresses the employer in a positive manner.

CONCLUSION

In looking back over what we have advised, we feel that the techniques and strategies used in counseling the disadvantaged do not diverge greatly from those used with advantaged persons. The primary consideration, then, becomes one of building trust between the middle-class group leader and the member. Once this rapport is developed, standard group techniques, as described, will work. An additional emphasis is that the customary definition of disadvantaged is too limited and should be more functional.

SELECTED READINGS

Amos, William E.: *Counseling the Disadvantaged Youth.* New York, Prentice-Hall, 1968.

Cull, John G., and Hardy, Richard E.: *Rehabilitation of the Urban Disadvantaged.* Springfield, Thomas, 1973.

Hardy, Richard E., and Cull, John G.: *Climbing Ghetto Walls.* Springfield, Thomas, 1973.

CHAPTER III

GROUP COUNSELING WITH PEOPLE WHO ARE MENTALLY HANDICAPPED

ROBERT A. LASSITER

INTRODUCTION

For our generation there is no such thing as life without trouble. There are only good kinds of trouble and bad kinds of trouble. How can we preserve our aspirations (without which no social betterment is possible) and at the same time develop the toughness of mind and spirit to face the fact that there are no easy victories.

John W. Gardner

The rehabilitation worker who is involved in the use of group counseling with people who are mentally handicapped—either at work in a facility or in a community based program—experiences "no easy victories". Gardner's usual skill in communicating a particular dilemma faced by the helping professions is applicable to the hundreds of rehabilitation workers who must choose, quite often, from alternatives in small group work that appear to be equally amorphous.

44

Three major difficult and perplexing problems are perceived by rehabilitation workers as they use small group methods in working with clients who are labeled as mentally handicapped:

1. A lack of solid evidence that group counseling produces a satisfactory work adjustment for people with serious mental problems.
2. Usually, an awkward or discomforting feeling on the part of the rehabilitation worker who assumes responsibility for group leadership; and, the accompanying anxiety and apprehension he experiences as he begins to interact with his clients.
3. An inability to apperceive a clear pattern of organization or a systematic framework within which the client and the counselor can work together toward the goal of freedom for the client through the medium of work.

PURPOSE OF THIS CHAPTER

The goal of this chapter is to examine these three areas of concern to the rehabilitation worker and the mentally handicapped client. First, a review of the professional literature is made. The purposes here are to assist in gaining historical perspective and to share in the search for circumstances which point to behavior, indicating group counseling may be beneficial. Second, a rationale for the role of the rehabilitation worker performing as a leader or facilitator in group counseling is presented in conjunction with a list of tentative requisites for prior experiences and training which appear to be needed by the rehabilitation worker in the field of mental health. And, third, general guidelines are postulated in an effort to offer rehabilitation personnel some assistance in the establishment of a systematic pattern to use in group counseling with people who suffer a variety of mentally handicapping conditions.

REVIEW OF THE LITERATURE

The use of group counseling or psychotherapy methods in the treatment of mental illness is not a new phenomenon to psychologists, psychiatrists, social workers, and other professional people involved in the rehabilitation process, in an institutional setting, or in a community mental health clinic. However, this approach or method has not been widely associated with the work of the rehabilitation counselor, work evaluator or other rehabilitation staff except in recent times (Rudd and Margolin, 1969). At the present time, group counseling is not only being chosen by large numbers of rehabilitation agencies and facilities as the *modus operandi* for staff to follow, but the increasing emphasis and importance placed on group work by the general public (and, particularly the "mental health public") has had a pervasive effect on the rehabilitation concept as it has emerged in the field of mental health in the past decade.

Walter Neff, in his book, *Work and Human Behavior,* chronicles the shift in rehabilitation techniques from "guidance" to "counseling" in more recent times as rehabilitation staff have turned to the problems of mentally handicapped people with severe conditions—which Neff states

> implies an increasing belief that the problems of adjustment to work are in some sense or other, problems of personality. Where these problems are severe, they cannot be solved by the giving of occupational information or the administration of tests. Some type of reconstruction of relevant areas of the personality appears to be required. The result has been an increasingly intensive search for appropriate methods of treatment (Neff, 1968).

One method found appropriate in this search appears to be group counseling. Despite the rapid, and at times excessive, production of explanations for group counseling, theoretical and philosophical definitions found in the literature are not very helpful to the rehabilitation worker. A major problem is the inability or unwillingness of leaders in the field of counseling to be more careful than they are in statements such as:

> Group counseling and group psychotherapy are treated as the same phenomenon except that each has a distinctive setting and a unique relationship to the network of persons in the group. Group counseling takes place largely in educational and social settings. Group psychotherapy is used in hospitals, clinics for mental health, and private practice by psychologists and psychiatrists (Fullmer, 1971).

Ohlsen attempts a similar distinction in his book, *Group Counseling,* by concluding "Group psychotherapy, on the other hand, is defined here as a therapeutic experience for emotionally disturbed persons . . ." (Ohlsen, 1970). While we can appreciate the contributions these authors and others are making in the search for a clear definition of group counseling and the distinctions between counseling and psychotherapy, these kinds of explanations are of no benefit to the rehabilitation counselor. Much of the rehabilitation worker's in-service and university education in counseling has provided a "role" for individual counseling based on the counseling model, i.e., the relationship found in the educational and social settings; and, while the rehabilitation practitioner and trainer have usually been able to modify theoretical constructs to fit the pragmatic world of rehabilitation—on the one-to-one relationship in counseling—it is clear that the rehabilitation counselor, for example, cannot follow this model in his work with small groups. The rehabilitation worker is, in reality, asked to conduct group counseling for the emotionally disturbed, the mentally retarded, and clients with serious behavior problems; in fact, these severely handicapped people represent the largest number of clients who now receive some type of group counseling services—from a task-oriented approach to a basic encounter or sensitivity activity. Thus, the clients themselves require a "different" type of group counseling. And, in addition, rehabilitation workers engaged in group work are employed as members of the "team" at a mental hospital, half-way or transitional living facility, or in a community mental health clinic—and, the professional models they find for group work would certainly be classified as "therapeutic".

A brief survey of rehabilitation training as shown in *The Use of Small Groups in Rehabilitation* suggests that universities and agency training staff have already turned to the basic encounter group or sensitivity training. In one chapter of this handbook, William Schutz, author of *Joy*, states, "Many of our methods come from areas loosely referred to as the human potential movement or the humanistic orientation . . ." (Berzon and Solomon, 1968). It is understatement to declare that this movement in training for rehabilitation workers in the more affective area of group work has presented serious problems to the rehabilitation practitioner who, with the client has the responsibility of maintaining a strongly goal-oriented approach to work adjustment, since *it* is the major component of the rehabilitation process.

As a result of confusion and frustration experienced in this area, it is important for rehabilitation administrators, facility and community rehabilitation staff, and university educators to begin looking seriously at the need for a more precise and parsimonious definition of what "rehabilitation group counseling" really is.

At this point, rehabilitation practitioners are coping with various ways to become involved with the feelings of clients, and at the same time they are emphasizing thoughts or behaviors that will lead to employment. These activities are attempts to blend the affective and cognitive areas in order to provide an opportunity for the mentally handicapped person to learn effective interpersonal and job skills. George Isaac Brown in his introduction to the concept of "confluent education" defines this blending as follows:

> Confluent education is the term for the integration of flowing together of the affective and cognitive elements in individual or **group learning** —sometimes called humanistic or psychological education . . . a philosophy and a process of learning in which the affective domain and the cognitive domain flow together, like two streams merging into one river, and are thus integrated in individual and group learning . . . It should be apparent that there is no intellectual learning without some sort of feeling, and there are no feelings without the mind's being somehow involved (Brown, 1971).

An important handbook distributed to rehabilitation workers in recent years is *Reality Coping and Employment Adjustment.* This approach to group counseling for mentally handicapped people is based on the concepts expressed by William Glasser in *Reality Therapy.* The "reality coping" goal in group counseling is viewed to be the learning by clients of effective rather than ineffective behaviors. "Needs are 'fulfilled' by the reinforcing properties of environmental conditions. Abilities are simply the responses utilized by the individual to respond to those aspects of his enviroment which require a 'coping' response. Congruence, then, between needs and environment reinforcing properties and congruence between patient abilities and the abilities required by the environment, will create realistic behavior" (Kramer and Hawkes, 1968).

In this reality coping approach to group counseling, the authors present two models which represent essentially what is to be taught conceptually to participants in a reality coping group. The first, *self improvement* is concerned with self-involvement, self-evaluation, self-direction, and self-achievement. These areas are "taught" to the participants in order for them to reach the goal of *self improvement*— "the emphasis is on *behavior in response to the environment,* i.e., being able to respond" (Kramer and Hawkes, 1968). In the second model, reality coping is portrayed as a set of concepts referred to as *action principles,* based on Glasser's reality therapy viewpoints. The action principle model produces a plan of action: It requires that group members become involved with others, and that changed behavior will result in changed feelings and emotions.

> This may begin in the group by constantly encouraging group members to support each other in desirable ways, to interact with telephone calls, or going to movies together between sessions, etc. Group members must be encouraged and then taught where necessary how to establish contacts with others . . . learning to function better will not be a mystery to group members. They can learn the concepts and learn them well (Kramer and Hawkes, 1968).

It appears that this model of reality coping and employment adjustment, while established specifically for post-hospital group counseling, contains principles and methods which can be adapted to the general guidelines that are recommended in the latter part of this chapter. And, the reality coping model, with modifications made by the rehabilitation worker to suit his own "reality", can be highly beneficial to group counseling with persons who are classified as mentally retarded.

In today's world of rehabilitation group counseling, the procedures or techniques used by the practitioner range *from* large group sessions (resembling classrooms), with members engaged in problem solving assignments under the supervision of a rehabilitation worker viewed as a teacher, a director of personnel, etc. *to* the small group approach based on Carl Rogers' basic encounter group, T-Group or sensitivity training, or other small group activities based in the affective area, with the rehabilitation worker acting as a group leader or facilitator who uses an extremely non-directive or group-centered attitude as well as technique (Rogers, 1970). In addition to the reality coping and employment adjustment handbook, there are several references available which include comprehensive descriptions of the great variety of small group methods now being used in rehabilitation and other settings. The T-Group or sensitivity training method developed by the National Training Laboratory in Bethel, Maine; the intensive or basic encounter approach of Carl Rogers established at the Center for the Studies of the Person at La Jolla, California; the rational-emotive marathon groups developed by Albert Ellis' institute in New York City; Big Sur, California's Esalen Institute which was influenced by Fritz Perls' gestalt therapy views; and other small group work which has had direct or indirect effects on the emerging process of rehabilitation group counseling are described in the following books:

T-Group Theory and Laboratory Methods, John Wiley and Sons, 1964. *Carl Rogers on Encounter Groups,* Carl Rogers, Harper and Row, 1970.
Group Counseling, Merle M. Ohlsen, Holt, Rinehart and Winston, 1970.
The Theory and Practice of Group Psychotherapy, Irwin D. Yalom, Basic Books, 1969.
The Use of Small Groups in Rehabilitation, Betty Berzon and Lawrence N. Solomon, Western Behavioral Sciences Institute, La Jolla, California, 1968.
Counseling, Group Theory and System, Daniel W. Fullmer, Intext Publishers, Scranton, Pennsylvania, 1971.
Encounter: Group Sensitivity Training Experience, Carl Goldberg, Science House, Inc., 1970.
Group Dynamics, Dorwin Cartwright and Alvin Zander, Harper and Row, 1968.
Groups, Gimmicks, and Instant Gurus, William R. Coulson, Harper and Row, 1972.

In concluding this general and admittedly somewhat limited survey of the literature which affects rehabilitation group counseling procedures, a statement made by Carl Rogers in a recent interview relates to rehabilitation agencies and facilities as they look to future possibilities in the movement toward greater use of the group counseling approach in rehabilitation (Rogers, 1972):

(Replying to a question regarding the future of encounter groups) I believe there will be possibilities for the rapid development of closeness between persons, a closeness which is not artificial, but, is real and deep, and which will be suited to our increasing mobility of living. Temporary relationships will be able to achieve the richness and meaning which heretofore have been associated only with life-long attachments. Aloneness will be something one chooses out of a desire for privacy, not an isolation into which one is forced.

Carl R. Rogers

RATIONALE FOR GROUP COUNSELING IN REHABILITATION

One achieves mental health to the extent that one becomes aware of one's interpersonal relationships.

Harry Stack Sullivan

For purposes of this chapter, group counseling in rehabilitation can be defined tentatively as the process in which the rehabilitation worker and a small group (eight to ten members) of clients work together in a rather flexible alliance of affective realms and the more cognitive fields related to action. This approach, combining the area of encounter-type sessions with action-oriented activities will allow mentally handicapped people an opportunity to acquire appropriate interpersonal skills as well as prepare for a more satisfactory adjustment to life through productive and self-actualizing behaviors— whether the process is designed for those clients with employment potential or for those who because of severity of disability, age, or other factors will perform limited work in activity centers or community programs in independent living.

"One of the major requirements of the adjustment to work is the ability to interact in certain appropriate ways with other people present on the scene" (Neff, 1968). Perhaps this thought expressed by Neff can provide rehabilitation workers with the best rationale for the use of small groups in workshops, centers, and other facilities. Existentialism appears to be the philosophical base for this "interaction with others on the scene" concept. For example, in almost all of the group counseling techniques there is the use of an ahistorical approach (the "here and now" views of Fritz Perls' gestalt therapy movement); participants are encouraged to interact on a feeling level, in an honest and open way—giving and receiving "feedback"; and the reliance on the climate of, and even the "personality" of the group for pressures to change rather than on authoritative pressure for the "right or wrong way". Arbuckle defines the existential psychologist's goal in therapy as one

to help the individual achieve a state of acceptance, of responsibility for self, thus to be free . . . Man is free—he is what he makes of himself, the "outside" limits and restricts [e.g., a handicapping condition], but it does not determine [completely] one's way of life. Existence precedes essence . . . Man is not static, but he is rather in a constant state of growing, evolving, becoming. He is in a state of being, but also non-being . . . Existentialism sees counseling and psychotherapy as primarily human encounter . . . The stress is on today rather than yesterday or tomorrow. A real human encounter must be in terms of now, and life and living are in terms of what *is,* not what was or what might be (Arbuckle, 1970).

Another hint of the origin of this philosophical base can be seen in Rollo May's statements:

Therapy is concerned with helping the person experience his existence as real . . . which includes becoming aware of his potentialities and becoming able to act on the basis of them . . . the significance of commitment is not that it is simply a vague good thing or ethically to be advised. It is a necessary prerequisite rather for seeing truth . . . decision precedes knowledge. We have worked normally on the assumption that, as the [clients] gets more and more knowledge and insight about himself, he will make appropriate decisions. This is a half truth. The second half of the truth is generally overlooked, namely, that the person cannot permit himself to get insight or knowledge until he is *ready* to decide, takes a decisive orientation to life and has made the preliminary decision along the way (May, 1958).

There is no question that rehabilitation personnel working with mentally handicapped people can benefit from a thorough study of an existentialist psychology since the rehabilitation concept itself is "an existentialist one". The thoughts expressed by Rollo May and others reinforce the choice made in rehabilitation toward group counseling as one way to help clients have the opportunity to interact with other people in order to make better decisions regarding adjustment to life and to work.

However, the rapidly proliferating group counseling approaches have brought problems to rehabilitation practitioners: the acceleration in group experiences and the prolific writings of research studies in the group process have resulted in a "knowledge explosion" which, in some cases, has prevented the practitioner from assimilating and implementing this knowledge. And, in turn, his frustration is increased by the demands of administrators, supervisors, university educators, and the clients themselves for an "instant movement" toward using more and more methods in group counseling—"whatever that means!"

Encounter groups distort what they are good at, which is a chance for a person to try himself out and make his own value discoveries . . . "You should say what you feel. Say it with directness. No need to hide here what would embarrass you elsewhere" Under that kind of pressure, a person might say and sometimes do considerably more than he means.

Encounter groups offend as dreadfully as any political collective, yet more immediately, when they roll along on the energy of a crowd, when they call on the individual to perform, when they become a court that decides about him and claims right of access to his secret heart. When that happens, I want no part of them.

Gimmicks are not necessary. The encounter can happen without them. So it bothers me when *groupers* haul them in. When a gimmick (or game) is going, one can't differentiate between what the gimmick makes happen and what *we* are able to achieve among ourselves.

These excerpts are taken out of context from *Groups, Gimmicks, and Instant Gurus, An Examination of Encounter Groups and Their Distortions* by William R. Coulson, a well-known and prominent leader in the development of encounter groups. He is a co-director of the "La Jolla Program", a group training center sponsored by Carl Rogers' Center for the Studies of the Person. Obviously, the man feels positively about the basic encounter approach to group therapy, and yet he expresses the concerns that many practitioners have felt about the intensive small group experience. In his book, he points out the flaws of the group process and at the same time provides his personal views of the benefits that "free" encounter sessions can provide: He asks, what has one achieved ideally, in encounter learning?

He [the client] has achieved an expanded range of choice. He can be more present to people when he wishes, and more private also when he wishes that. He can be in charge of his life through being more aware of where he is; that is to say, less compelled by his habits, with less need to defend against his experience, with greater sensitivity to the full range of feelings all people have. One of the interesting facts about the long-run effects of encounter groups is that, after going through the considerable kinds of trauma I have been describing, individuals often wind up looking much as they did before the encounter. But with a difference. I know it in my own life: this time I can choose to be the way I am, and I can sense in myself the real possibility to be other than how typically I am, *if I judge that to be appropriate*. I am no longer compelled to be some one way. One could not ask for more (Coulson, 1972). Just as one could not ask more of the person who is mentally handicapped and is working toward a new adjustment to life and work.

Charles B. Truax of the Arkansas Rehabilitation Research and Training Center, comments on the group process in rehabilitation:

> . . . there is abundant evidence available indicating that genuineness (honesty and realism), warmth and interpersonal contact, and empathy or listening for the person inside the other are indeed significant sources for therapeutic personality and behavioral change . . . While we at present do in fact have more research evidence, both solid and suggestive, than is being utilized in practice or in training, it is also clear that research will forever lag behind innovation in practice . . . I would like to reiterate the importance of *outcome* research over *process* research. In a sense, our training institutions, state licensing boards, and professional board examinations have also been process rather than outcome oriented. In view of the mounting evidence demonstrating conclusively that the practice of [group] counseling and psychotherapy is, on the average, ineffective, a focus on therapeutic outcome is vital to the development of our field (Traux, 1968).

In the development of a rationale for the role of the rehabilitation worker to perform effectively as a leader or facilitator in group counseling, it seems important to review the critiques by Coulson and other group leaders on how group counseling is being distorted and sometimes abused; and equally important to study carefully the comments and suggestions made by counseling leaders such as Truax in regard to research—"outcome" research or a study of what happens to our clients after group counseling is completed is not only a more realistic approach in research in this field, but it is one that students working in a practicum in a university setting and rehabilitation workers in the field can perform without a great deal of excess work in the office and without the expert skill and knowledge required in process research.

> With regard to it (the theory of relativity) science and research owe much to intuition and to "being sympathetically in touch with experience"—I came to it by continuing to ask myself questions about space and time that only children ask.
>
> Albert Einstein

It is difficult to answer the question posed by many practitioners in the rehabilitation field in regard to minimum qualifications for counselors and other personnel who work with mentally handicapped people in small groups. *Assuming* that the professional person assigned to group work or who is responsible for setting up group experiences for clients has already met the "generally accepted standards" for performance as a rehabilitation professional person and that he has an understanding and accepting attitude toward his clients—and toward the disability label, too—then the following suggestions are made:

1. A master's degree in a rehabilitation field or its equivalent (as indicated in recent certification statements made by the National Association of Rehabilitation Counseling).
2. At least one experience as a member of a basic encounter or sensitivity training group.
3. One or two introductory courses in social psychology emphasizing the research studies in group dynamics.
4. Selection of a consultant (or co-leader)—one who has wide experience in group work and possesses a positive professional reputation among his peers—in other words, "check him out"— a Ph.D. is not, in itself, a reliable criterion for selecting a competent supervisor or consultant in this field.
5. *Read* all books, articles in professional journals, reports of conferences, etc. which are available.

(The dilemma here: there are professional people who are extremely effective in group work who may not meet all of these suggested "requisites"; and, there are rehabilitation workers who meet all the above suggestions for competency, and have additional "credentials" who are not successful in helping clients through this approach.)

Before we begin to look to the development of general guidelines for establishing some systematic pattern to follow in the use of small groups with mentally handicapped people, a final statement is taken from an article appearing in *Rehabilitation Record,* "Group Counseling with Rehabilitation Clients" (Gust, 1970).

While I would not call it a panacea, group counseling—both leaderless and counselor-led—appears to offer to the rehabilitation client the opportunity to learn to adjust to his role as a handicapped person through an experience in positive social interaction for long-term usefulness. In rehabilitation we are concerned with some type of reintroduction of the client into the typically able-bodied or nonhandicapped community. This is one common bond which most rehabilitation clients share. (And), there are many other common concerns for the handicapped client which makes group counseling an appropriate choice . . . Being able to experience and work through real feelings encountered in group interaction is probably the most unique and beneficial aspect of group as compared with individual counseling.

Tim Gust

A PATTERN TO USE IN GROUP COUNSELING IN REHABILITATION SETTINGS

This pattern of organization of small group work in rehabilitation will require modification by the practitioner to meet the reality of his particular work situation. While the plan is based on empirical studies and abstract philosophical theses, "outcome" research suggested by Truax is limited to one experience altered to meet specific needs of a group of students; therefore, the activity schedule should be viewed by the group leader as a flexible guide and *not* a formal plan that has received the blessings of "process" research—in fact, at this point, it is perhaps more important for rehabilitation workers to remain open to the group movement and while using the group method, follow Truax's suggestion of each student and practitioner utilizing an "outcome" research plan. This practice can be beneficial not only to the rehabilitation group leader; but, if shared with others, it can provide the basis for an orderly, evolving systematic approach which can help more mentally handicapped people become productive.

Outline of an Activity Schedule

One Week — During the first week, eight to ten mentally handicapped people are selected for group membership
Rehabilitation worker and client meet in individual conferences for orientation
Rehabilitation worker distributes the plan to all concerned.
First meeting of the group devoted to instruction related to small group dynamics

Four Weeks — Four encounter type small group sessions—one hour per week for the four-week period

One Week — Individual conferences with clients—thirty minutes to one hour each for the one-week period

Three Weeks   Three task-oriented or problem solving sessions—one hour per week for this three-week period

One Week   *A Plan* is prepared by the client and the rehabilitation worker related to adjustment to employment—through individual conferences—thirty minutes to one hour each for the one-week period

Total:
Ten Weeks

I. *Introduction:*

A. The rehabilitation worker arranges for eight to ten clients to meet in a small group setting. One hour per week for the group counseling, and thirty minutes to one hour per individual session. This allows for seven weeks of one hour group counseling sessions and three weeks for personal interviews.

B. The rehabilitation worker interviews each client selected for the program during the first week as the schedule begins. Participants are told in this conference about the overall plan for the group and individual meetings, the meeting place, time, others involved, and the specific reason for the use of the group approach. Each client has an opportunity to clarify for himself the purpose of the small group work and the rehabilitation worker will be able to gather new data about the individual which may help to facilitate the client's learning about himself in relation to others in the world of work.

C. Also, in the first week of the schedule, the rehabilitation worker should inform all administrators and colleagues of the plan and have copies of the schedule of activities distributed to other members of the staff. It is important for the counselor to make clear the need for maintaining confidentiality in regard to the group sessions and to explain the importance of this "keeping quiet" attitude until each client, with the assistance of the group leader, prepares and distributes a progress report on himself to all staff, other agency professional personnel, or to employers (at the end of the sessions).

D. One final activity is suggested for the facilitator during this first week of the activity schedule: (The term facilitator will be used for the rehabilitation worker during the remainder of this schedule.) This final preliminary action will require that the facilitator set up a one hour meeting of all participants (this follows the individual conferences). The purpose of this meeting is to teach clients what group counseling is: to review the schedule, to give an explanation of what is expected by participants, and what role or roles the facilitator will play. If video or audio equipment is being considered for use in the groups, it will be wise for the facilitator to receive a group consensus on this as well as any other technical concerns. In this initial meeting, the group members are receiving instruction from the facilitator, and the climate should resemble an "open classroom" type of session. If honesty and openness is to come later, it's extremely important that the facilitator be honest about the purpose: "It's to help you adjust to work," for example. Also, the facilitator should share with the group all the "secret and mysterious things" about group dynamics which he or she has learned (dependent in degree, of course, on the ability of the clients to understand). Every effort should be made to avoid burdening the group members with the facilitator's problem of "wearing two hats—teacher and facilitator". The facilitator is encouraged to say that "sometimes I will be there as your counselor, and I will do most of the listening in order for you to speak and listen to each other about the way you feel—and, later I will be a more active participant as we begin to work on specific problems regarding your plans for employment or training." And, of course, the facilitator should inform the clients of his own pledge of confidentiality. This informal meeting of the group should provide the facilitator with additional background information about the group members in order to plan for a ten-week schedule that will be uniquely suitable. And last, it is important for the

facilitator to avoid during these first meeings a manipulative approach—be honest. For example, if direction is
needed in your judgment, give it; but, watch for and
avoid the more subtle "guarded and hidden" manipulative stance.

II. Small Group Activity—Phase I (First four weeks of encounter
approach—one hour per session)

An opportunity is provided for clients to follow the basic encounter
approach in group work—for each client to develop interpersonal
skills with other members, with the facilitator encouraging clients to
be sensitive to feelings and to speak openly about them (if they so
desire!). Certain exercises from books on enounter work, cassette
tapes, and other programmed instruction in interpersonal behavior
may be helpful to "new" practitioners (especially in working with
people who are retarded). These aids are intended as *temporary*
devices to assist the facilitator in establishing early a climate of trust
and openness in this particular phase of the plan. Coulson cautions
us to be wary of these "gimmicks"—and, who can be *for* gimmicks?
A *gimmick* is defined as an "ingenious or novel device, scheme, de-
ception or hidden disadvantage" *(Random House Dictionary,* 1968).
However, the first part of the definition parallels the definition for
gadget: "a mechanical contrivance or device; any ingenious article"
(Random House Dictionary, 1968). Gadgets appear to be justified
only when they are used on a temporary basis and *only* when they
are carefully selected to avoid what Coulson calls "making things
happen that the group itself can achieve". In this phase of the small
group activity, clients are encouraged to stay with the "here and
now" attitude within the group. The facilitator can assist the group
in looking at strengths rather than weaknesses. Successful group
counseling in this first four week period would mean that each client
experiences:

greater acceptance of his total being—emotional, intellectual, and
physical—as it *is,* including its potential . . . [appreciates that] individuals can hear each other, can learn from each other, to a greater
extent; [the value of] feedback from one person to another, such that each

individual learns how he appears to others and what impact he has in interpersonal relationships . . . [that] the learnings in the group experience tend to carry over, temporarily or more permanently in relationships with [others in different settings] (Rogers, 1970).

III. Individual Counseling Sessions—Phase II (One week for personal interviews between the facilitator and individual clients—thirty minutes to one hour)

This week of individual conferences can be viewed as a bridge between the more "affective" area of group work which was experienced in the four week encounter sessions and the more "cognitive" area of group work which will be emphasized in the three problem solving sessions to follow. There are two major purposes for these interviews which "interrupt" the group counseling process:

1. the client has an opportunity to share privately any feelings and concerns about his experience in the earlier group sessions—he may feel uncomfortable or embarrassed about his "openness" or that of others.

2. the client has the opportunity to share privately any new ideas he may have about himself or his plans for adjustment to work.

Also, the facilitator at this point can review briefly plans for the more structured, problem solving group sessions and, in some cases, he may assign a task for the client to work out prior to or during the group counseling.

IV. Small Group Activity—Phase III (For the next three week— one hour per session in group counseling)

The purpose of Phase III in this activity schedule for use of group counseling in rehabilitation is to begin to focus on general work skills that are common to all jobs. The tasks to be assigned to the group will relate to learning ways of becoming effective workers in the real world of work. Some of the assignments made by the facilitator in these three more cognitive or task-oriented sessions will include:

A. *First Assignment*

Each group member will share with the group the problems that he is experiencing in whatever work situation in which he has been involved, either in prevocational or work evaluation settings, or job-tryouts, etc. These problems may have to do with attitudes toward employers, fellow employees, work habits, and other basic problems involved with the work setting. "Feedback" from others will be the key in these sessions.

B. *Second Assignment*

Each client will share with the group his own self-evaluation. A form can be devised by the facilitator to ask for a listing of strengths and weaknesses, including a statement at the end such as "what I can do to build on my strengths and find ways to eliminate or accept my weaknesses in order to become a free person with productive work?"

C. *Third Assignment*

Each client will share with the group *a plan* he has set up by himself (at times, with the help of the facilitator, if required). The plan will indicate how he plans to assume responsibility for getting a job, a job-tryout, an on-the-job experience, or some kind of vocational training. In addition, each client will be asked to share his evaluation of the group experience and to share his thoughts and feelings about himself and his future.

(these three assignments are set up to provide for a "main topic" for each of the three task-oriented group counseling sessions as scheduled above)

V. Individual Counseling Sessions—Phase IV (One week for personal interviews between the facilitator and individual clients—thirty minutes to one hour each)

In an attempt to integrate the group counseling method into the total mental health and rehabilitation process, this last week of the activity schedule is designed to provide an opportunity for the facilitator to have an individual conference with each member of the group. The results of this interview will constitute a "joint communiqué" type of progress report in which the client and the facilitator sit down together and work out a report to be distributed to staff members and others who might be concerned with the clients adjustment to work or other activities. This report can be made in the form of a recommendation, e.g., "It is recommended that this person participate in additional work adjustment programs; or, enter an activity type program not involved with competitive employment; or, take vocational training; or become employed, etc."

This completes the pattern of organization. Activities that are involved with the feelings of clients and those that are emphasizing thoughts that will lead to action are viewed as a blending of these two areas (affective and cognitive) which will provide an opportunity for the mentally handicapped person to learn better how to adjust to the job.

> Group therapy has had a succession of attractive wrappings: it was, during World War II, the economical answer to a shortage of trained therapists; later it became a logical treatment arena of the interpersonal theory of psychology; and currently is it a medium for alleviating individual and social alienation. At present, groups, self-disclosure, interpersonal closeness, touching are "in". Yet the medium is *not* the message. Group [counseling] is not primarily a vehicle for closeness and human contact. It is a method for effecting therapeutic change in individuals. All other goals are metaphenomena and secondary to the primary function of the group.
>
> Irwin D. Yalom

GUIDELINES IN THE USE OF GROUP COUNSELING WITH MENTALLY RETARDED PEOPLE

As Rick Heber points out in the book he edited, *Special Problems in Vocational Rehabilitation of the Mentally Retarded,*

> The counseling process for mentally retarded clients is *essentially the same* as for all disabled persons. As with all developmental disabilities, lifelong experiences of failure and rejection often create particularly difficult rehabilitation problems which can only be resolved through personal counseling. The intellectual limitations of the retarded client, and particularly his deficit in verbal communication, do necessitate modifications in usual counseling techniques and require the utilization of a wider range of approaches (Heber, 1965).

In addition to these problems that mentally retarded people experience, other difficulties are experienced when a group counseling method is used by the rehabilitation worker. For example, in a study of techniques for predicting vocational success of mentally retarded adults conducted by the Human Resources Center in Albertson, New York, the work of the project director and his research associates shows the special problems and also the promises of the use of the group approach: "The relative importance of personal-social factors and specific skill factors depends on the nature of the job as well as the level of skill required in the job. It has been suggested that the lower the skill level required in the job, the more important become the personal-social factors. In other words, if little or no skill is required for a job, the only criterion for continued employability is the personal-social factor" (Manus, Kovacs, Roberts, and Levy, 1970). As Henry Viscardi writes in the foreword of this research study, "Although the findings must be preliminary, they do suggest directions in the rehabilitation of the mentally retarded client that have been previously neglected or ignored. . ." (Manus, Kovacs, Roberts, and Levy, 1970). And, because of the special problems encountered in the field of mental retardation, there has been a reluctance to provide a rehabilitation group counseling setting for people who are mentally retarded. Yet, we know that mentally retarded people have been able to meet certain personal, social, and vocational needs through counseling. George Baroff, a leader in the rehabilitation field of mental retardation, states: "Retarded individuals, like the rest of us, share needs for survival, structure, self-esteem, and self-expression. While the disability of mental retardation does not affect basic needs, qualitatively, it does influence their relative intensity and the likelihood of their being met" (Hardy and Cull, 1973). Most sheltered workshop and facility programs appear to have accepted these basic needs as expressed by Baroff or at least have given emphasis to similar models of *what* the retarded person needs; special projects in this field almost always report on the efforts to effect change in personal and social behaviors. But rarely have reports of these projects or observation of facilities shown the exploration into the area of group counseling as a formal procedure useful to the rehabilitation of persons who are retarded.

One research and demonstration project that does report on its use of the small group approach is the project mentioned earlier which was carried out at Viscardi's Human Resources Center and Abilities Inc. program on Long Island.

The following impressions were derived from utilization of group counseling techniques as a component of the total rehabilitation project:

1. Great reluctance on the part of the clients to talk about topics with emotional content—reflecting a general mistrust initially of the group leader.

2. Once the initial reluctance was overcome for many, it was noted that several members continued to remain silent—a factor attributed to anxiety over handling "excessive input", as seen in one member's question: "What do I do if everybody answers me at once?"

3. It appeared to the researchers that some members who remained silent had experienced more negative reactions to their attempts at verbalization in the past, and under such circumstances, their reluctant verbal behaviors might be as much a reflection of continuing negative expectations of others as any inherent lack of ability to communicate.

4. Through serendipity, they found that the reduction in group size in one group experience overcame the problems experienced earlier relative to verbalization: "With the reduction of the group to four members and a leader, the remaining counselees embarked on lengthy discussions of feelings previously avoided. . . The small group size seemed to lessen the fear of 'excessive input' and eliminated the 'classroom' feeling. As one of the trainees put it: 'The meetings were sort of like a family get-together' ".

5. Early in the group counseling sessions, it became apparent that coping with the label "retardation" and the loneliness prominent in many of the clients' daily lives were deterrents to acceptance of realistic vocational goals (Manus, Kovacs, Roberts and Levy, 1970).

Since the findings of this study are in general agreement with other project reports related to the use of group counseling for persons who are retarded and experience and observation would indicate some reliable inference can be obtained from its logic, much of the modified activity schedule which follows reflects the impressions derived from this and similar observations.

As can be noted, the changes made in the outline of the schedule are mostly quantitative which also provides for greater emphasis in certain areas, e.g., orientation and instruction. It would not be accurate to assume the changes are due entirely to the need for "slow" learners to have more time, nor that there is more time available to the rehabilitation worker because of fewer group members; however, consideration has been given to these areas. The major reason for the changes center around the fact that most mentally retarded people will be employed in jobs that will require less technical skills—but *more* interpersonal skills. This concept of group work for retarded people also encompasses the more specific problems demonstrated in the Human Resources Center's study: greater reluctance to speak openly of emotions; initially, a general mistrust of the group facilitator; anxiety on the part of clients caused by a feeling of "excessive input"; minimum verbal behavior reflecting the continuing negative expectation of others of what the retarded person says; the unrealistic goals of retarded people in regard to employment, etc.

Reduction of the size of the group from eight to ten members to only four with the group approach for mentally retarded people— the major change—appears to be indicated in order to minimize or eliminate the problems listed above. In reviewing the more detailed pattern of organization recommended for group counseling with emotionally disturbed or mentally handicapped people, all other activities appear to be compatible with the needs of persons who are retarded, with one exception: it is anticipated that the rehabilitation worker will be required to become more directive in assisting the client in developing the *plan,* with greater attention paid to external evaluative processes.

The schedule developed earlier in this chapter to offer a general guideline to follow in rehabilitation group counseling remains substantially intact; however, a few alterations are required to meet the more special needs of people who are mentally retarded. Five steps were outlined to convey the series of events occurring in the ten-week schedule:

(Changes or modifications of the original plan are underlined)

I.
    1. During the first week, four mentally retarded people are selected for the group counseling experience.
    2. The rehabilitation worker meets with the client in an individual counseling session for orientation and instruction.

One Week	3. A copy of the total plan is distributed to all members of the staff, including the administrative personnel.
	4. The first meeting of the group is called and the counselor assumes the role of a teacher—to instruct the four member groups in goals of group counseling.
II.	Four encounter-type small group sessions will be held—two hours per week for the four week period. (Two hours may
Four Weeks	be divided into shorter segments during the week.)
III.	Individual conferences with clients for feedback and additional orientation—one to two hours for each client during the one-week period.
IV.	Three task-oriented or problem solving group sessions—two hours per week for the three week period. (Two hours may
Three Weeks	be divided into shorter segments during the week.)
V.	Progress report and plan prepared by the client and the rehabilitation worker through individual counseling sessions
One Week	—one to two hours each for the one-week period.

SUMMARY

This chapter focuses on three major areas of concern as perceived by rehabilitation practitioners in accepting responsibility for leading or facilitating small groups whose members are mentally handicapped. These concerns include the lack of solid evidence that group counseling does produce satisfactory work adjustment for people with serious mental problems; the rehabilitation worker's anxiety and apprehension in regard to his new role as a group leader; and the lack of general guidelines that can offer a model or pattern to the rehabilitation staff. An attempt is made to provide a review of the literature demonstrating positive results of research and concepts developed by the various leaders in the group movement. This review also contains notes of caution and constructive criticisms from leaders in the field. Following the survey, an effort is made to offer a rationale for the rehabilitation worker's role in group counseling with mentally handicapped people. And, a pattern is formulated for use by the practitioner in the establishment of an activity schedule for beginning group work. In a final special section of the chapter, guidelines are suggested for adapting the activity schedule of rehabilitation group counseling methods to the needs of people who are mentally retarded.

REFERENCES

Arbuckle, Dugald S.: *Counseling: Philosophy, Theory and Practice.* Boston, Allyn and Bacon, 1970.

Berzon, Betty, and Solomon, Lawrence N.: *The Use of Small Groups in Rehabilitation.* Western Behavioral Sciences Institute, La Jolla, California, 1968.

Brown, George Issac: *Human Teaching for Human Learning, An Introduction to Confluent Education.* New York, Viking, 1971.

Coulson, William R.: *Groups, Gimmicks, and Instant Gurus,* New York, Harper and Row, 1972.

Fullmer, Daniel W.: *Counseling—Group Theory and System.* Scranton, International Textbook, 1971.

Gardner, John W.: *No Easy Victories.* New York, Harper and Row, 1968.

Glasser, William: *Reality Therapy.* New York, Harper and Row, 1965.

Gust, Tim: Group counseling with rehabilitation clients. *Rehabilitation Record,* January-February, 1970.

Hardy, Richard E., and Cull, John G.: *Vocational Evaluation for Rehabilitation Services.* Springfield, Thomas, 1973.

Heber, Rick (Ed.): *Vocational Rehabilitation of the Mentally Retarder.* Rehabilitation Services Series, No. 65-16, U.S. Department of Health, Education, and Welfare, 1965.

Kramer, Elmer E., and Hawkes, F. James: *Reality Coping and Employment Adjustment: A Handbook for Post-Hospital Group Counseling,* Colorado State University, Fort Collins, Colorado, 1968.

Manus, Gerald I., Kovacs, Marika, Roberts, Norman, and Levy, Barbara: *Skill Analysis as Technique for Predicting Vocational Success of the Mentally Retarded.* Human Resources Center, Albertson, New York, 1970.

May, Rollo: Contributions of existential psychotherapy. *Existence,* New York, Simon and Schuster, 1958.

Neff, Walter S.: *Work and Human Behavior.* New York, Atherton, 1968.

Ohlsen, Merle M.: *Group Counseling.* New York, Holt, Rinehart and Winston, 1970.

Rogers, Carl R.: *Carl Rogers on Encounter Groups.* New York, Harper and Row, 1970.

Rogers, Carl R.: *Human Behavior,* I, November-December, 1972

Rudd, Jacob L. and Margolin, Reuben J.: *Rehabilitation Medicine—Psychiatric.* West Medford, R.M.D., 1969.

Sullivan, Harry Stack: *Conceptions of Modern Psychiatry.* New York, W.W. Norton, 1940.

The Random House Dictionary of the English Language. New York, Random House, 1968.

CHAPTER IV

GROUP COUNSELING
WITH PUBLIC OFFENDERS

RICHARD E. HARDY AND JOHN G. CULL

Who Is the Public
  Offender?
What Is Group Counseling
  and Therapy?
Client Characteristics
Qualification for Group
  Counseling Work

Grouping Inmates
Goals of Group Counseling
Group Leadership Methods
Summary
Some Basic Assumptions
  in Counseling

C OUNSELING HAS BEEN used as a tool in various therapeutic settings mainly on an individual or one-to-one basis. Recent research (Gazda, 1970) has indicated that not only can counseling be done in groups, but there is considerable therapeutic value in the interaction among members of an intimate group. Since professional therapeutic staff in prisons are in short supply and group counseling has been shown to be highly effective, it is only natural that the process of group counseling be tried in various correctional settings.

WHO IS THE PUBLIC OFFENDER?

Delinquent or criminal acts are committed by people at all levels in the society. There is no class of criminals versus non-criminals. There is a group of the "caught" versus the "non-caught".

We can ascertain from the study of arrest records, probation reports, and other statistics related to penal systems that the offender is an individual who has been disadvantaged in education and mental and physical health. He is likely to be a member of the lower social and economic group who is poorly educated, underemployed, probably unmarried, a product of a broken home, and more than likely has a prior criminal record.

The stereotyping of public offenders just as that of other individuals is a dangerous procedure and this should be carefully noted. Not all offenders fit any composite profile. We must remember that the portrait of the offender just described is taken from those who have been arrested, tried, and sentenced. Many persons, as previously indicated, who are guilty of crime are not included in the portrait. Statistics based on national arrest records indicate that when all offenses are considered together the majority of offenders are over 24 years of age, white, male. The great majority of persons arrested for fraud, embezzlement, gambling, drunkenness, offenses against the family, and vagrancy are over 24 years of age. The younger group, those 15 to 17, are the ones who commit the most burglaries, larcenies, and auto thefts. Statistics show that males are arrested nearly seven times more frequently than females. (Institute on Rehabilitation Services, 1969)

In terms of the socio-economic family dimensions of offenders, it can be said that often the person is a homeless male, single, divorced, separated, or likely to have had an unstable marriage. He is highly mobile, having probably recently changed his residence. He may very well be a member of a minority group and have experienced cultural deprivation. He probably is dependent on public welfare or some other type of financial aid. Intelligence appears to be fairly normally distributed in the offender population, but education is not. Offenders have less education than the general population. Getting work is a major problem for this group of people and keeping work once it is attained is an additional problem.

In terms of psychological aspects, the offender often is a person who has isolated himself somewhat from others. He tends to be suspicious and to "act out" or has difficulty controlling his impulses. He often tends to be a hypermanic or over-active type of person. He may have difficulty in planning his activities and thinking out various alternative approaches for action. Often there is considerable hostility. In addition, offenders may have problems with alcoholism, sexual deviance, and narcotics addiction. The number who are emotionally disturbed and mentally ill is significant.

Group counseling can probably be of particular value to the offender soon after he is incarcerated. After remaining in the penal system for some time, he will become accustomed to the institutional way of life and group counseling or any other type of counseling is hampered. Toward the end of the inmate's stay in prison, group or individual counseling again has a better chance for success since he is planning on getting himself ready for the outside world and is more receptive than when he is in the middle of a long stay in a penal institution.

WHAT IS GROUP COUNSELING AND THERAPY?

According to Moreno (1962) "group psychotherapy" means simply to treat people in groups. A composite definition of group counseling has been presented by Gazda. "Group counseling is a dynamic interpersonal process focusing on conscious thought and behavior and involving the therapy functions of permissiveness, orientation to reality, catharsis and mutual trust, caring, understanding, acceptance, and support. The therapy functions are creative and nurtured in a small group through the sharing of personal concerns with one's peers and the counselor(s)".

The group counselees are basically normal individuals with various concerns which are not debilitating to the extent requiring extensive personality change. The counselees will utilize the group interaction to increase understanding and acceptance of values and goals and to learn and/or unlearn certain attitudes and behaviors (Gazda, Duncan, Meadows, 1967).

In group counseling the leader of the group attempts to get members involved in various relationships in order that his (the leader's) role can be reduced. The leader functions by reflecting the feelings as he interprets them of others and giving meaning to what is said by all members of the group. The leader serves as a catalyst in helping different members of the group understand fully what is said or felt by other members of the group. He minimizes differences in perceptions by helping to explain the thoughts and feelings of others. He reflects the general feeling of the group.

Of course, he must initially establish certain rules covering the behavior of the group in terms of confidentiality, the general requirements of group members, etc. The group leader often varies his role according to the needs of the group. He may function as facilitator, resource person, or client. Above all, he constantly demonstrates his feeling of warmth, and genuine positive regard and respect for the honestly given perceptions and reactions of each member. He provides them a role model which group members may use during the group session.

CLIENT CHARACTERISTICS

The client must be open and genuine. He must honestly and genuinely seek to improve his adjustment by understanding his behavior and the reactions of other persons toward him. Truax (1961) reports that as the genuineness of group members in the psychotherapy relationship increases, so does the amount of depth of intra-personal exploration, the development of insight, and the rate of personal references.

One of the problems which exists in working with clients in penal institutions centers around the fact that they are involuntarily in residence. These persons must understand the therapeutic effects of group counseling to wish to open themselves from the point of view of reviewing personal inadequacies in order to improve their adjustment. If they are permitted to participate for a long enough period to experience basic therapeutic effects, they often will feel much less defensive. The counselor must allow persons who wish to leave the group and not participate to do so.

Counseling in therapy groups does not have the highly defined group goals as may be wished for in vocational advising or counseling. The emphasis is on effective, honest communication. Group counseling is much more goal oriented than is group therapy. In school settings and similar group settings, goals can be somewhat specific. The counselor will always have to remember that no matter how well individuals accept general goals of the group, the client's goals are always his own.

QUALIFICATIONS FOR GROUP COUNSELING WORK

First of all, the group counselor must have a genuine and sympathetic interest in other human beings in order to be effective. He must be a stable individual of considerable insight and maturity. He must have considerable knowledge of psychology and interhuman processes.

Along with these characteristics go appropriate attitudes which allow the group leader to work with inmates of minority groups and the ability to handle hostility when inmates direct it at him or other group members. A very important characteristic is knowing when one is in "over his head" in group work and when to request help from individuals more sensitive or competent.

The group leader's role is quite difficult. It requires considerable study, practical types of experience, and a high degree of personal development.

The inmate must be willing to trust the group leader. The leader must be recognized by them as one who will not betray them and he must be able to accept members of the group no matter what their status in life is or their level of adjustment.

The novice in group work, whether he plans to be a lay leader or later a professional group worker, must recognize that there is a substantial body of knowledge to be mastered. He must also recognize the need for supervision by persons trained in group work, and he will wish to participate as a group member under the leadership of a highly trained person before deciding he is ready to take on the leadership of the group.

Group work with inmates can be very rewarding. At times it will be difficult to see whether or not progress is being made, and in some cases, inmates will notice growth behavior in others before the group leader becomes aware of this phenomenon. As inmates become better adjusted, they will become more friendly toward other inmates and staff persons. They will be more interested in their previous friends and family. They will react more effectively interpersonally among their peers. Some inmates will take on leadership responsibilities within the group. Group leaders should not become overly concerned in attempting to measure change or progress in his group. This measurement will be particularly difficult in the early days of the group meetings when it is probably most necessary for the group leader to see that he is accomplishing some goals. The leader should expect no rapid changes in behavior. He should just continue his group meetings in an atmosphere of acceptance—refraining at all times from authoritarianism.

Differences in Group Counseling and Group Psychotherapy

Group psychotherapy is at a more advanced stage in its development than is group counseling. Group counseling usually is oriented toward the Adlerian client-centered or eclectic. Stefflre in his *Theories of Counseling* (1965), has said that "indeed, most theorists in the field would agree that counseling is a learning process, although there they may have sharp differences as to what facilitates learning and how learning occurs". According to Gazda (1970), group counseling and group psychotherapy lie on a continuum with an overlapping of goals and professional competencies, but the subtle distinctions are evident in expressions such as "basically normal counselees" focusing on conscious thought, behavior, and concerns which are not debilitating to the extent requiring extensive personality change. Counseling is usually described as supportive, situational, and educational in terms of conscious awareness and of a short-term nature. Psychotherapy has been characterized as reconstructive, in-depth and analytical with an emphasis on the unconscious, the neurotic, and the severe emotional problems. Psychotherapy is thought of as being of a long-term nature. Traux (1961), reported that group cohesiveness was one of three group conditions significantly related to interpersonal exploration. It is extremely important for a cooperative group spirit to exist and there must be empathy among all the clients. Traux has also stated that the group is perhaps more potent in its effects on interpersonal exploration than is the therapist.

GROUPING INMATES

Often, it will be necessary for the counselor to experiment with trial placements in groups since it is difficult to know how given individuals will react once they are in a specific group. After several group meetings, the permanency of groups can be established by shifting persons from one group to another. The counselor may want to start with twice as many members in a group as he wants and then divide the group according to the members who seem to fit together in a way which will be most conducive to achieving maximum therapeutic usefulness of the group.

In conducting groups within penal settings, the counselor or therapist will often find that participants are hostile and involuntary. Corsini, (1957) has shown that clients can become much more accepting of the group through the technique of the counselor's demonstration of understanding and his reflection of the reason for their hostile feelings.

The research on homogeneous versus heterogeneous groupings has given us little to use in terms of knowing which is most effective. When persons are in homogeneous groups in terms of personality structure, each group member often tends to reinforce another's pattern of behavior. Heterogeneous groups seem to give more learning material to the group as a whole and for this reason heterogeneous groups may be more effective. Certainly groups cannot consist of all aggressive, dominating, or shy persons or all persons with psychopathic personalities if groups are to be effective and people are to learn from one another.

The counselor will wish to hold a diagnostic screening interview with each perspective counselee. This will be necessary so that persons can be screened in and out of the grouping experience and so that individuals who are about to join the group will understand how the group operates. They can then make a decision concerning whether they wish to become a member of the group or not. Once the group has begun, it is the responsibility of the leader to explain such matters as confidentiality, attendance, and the right of the leader to remove a person from a group and set certain structures concerning meals, use of bathroom facilities, etc.

GOALS OF GROUP COUNSELING

The group leader must remember that if group counseling is to be effective, it must be a growth experience for the inmate. The inmate must move toward developing from the point of view of maturing of attitudes toward himself and toward others. He must ask himself the question, "What will life consist of in future days?" The answer is often only his to give.

Group counseling should provide an inmate the opportunity to learn about his own individual personality and how it serves him in his relationships with others. He should be helped to understand any unrealistic, fantasy, or day-dreaming behavior that reflects his general adjustment. He must understand the price that he must pay for various types of behavior. Group counseling should offer inmates an opportunity to evaluate and study their own feelings and beliefs and those of others in a constructive group setting. In groups, inmates should be allowed to "spill out" with impunity their hostilities and painful experiences in order that their anxiety may be reduced. One of the substantial advantages of group counseling and therapy is that persons realize their problems are not unique. Other inmates have had the same problematic situation. Group counseling should help the inmate in his adjustment within the institution and improve his ability to adjust once he is outside the institution. Generally, it should improve relationships between staff and inmates within the prison by helping inmates to maintain self-control and develop attitudes of acceptance toward other inmates and prison personnel.

The purpose of group counseling and therapy in prison is not the prevention of escapes or elimination of various in-house troubles; but its main purpose is that of treatment—getting the inmates ready to return to society.

GROUP LEADERSHIP METHODS

1. Upon the initial meeting of the group, join them as a member. Take no immediate leadership role.
2. Introduce yourself once the group has started by giving your name and any other information you wish to give about yourself.
3. Ask the inmates to introduce themselves and say something briefly about themselves.
4. If you are asked the purpose of the group, you may wish to say that it is simply to help everyone become better adjusted, not only to prison life, but to life on the outside once they are released.
5. The leader must convince the members of the confidentiality of of the various sessions. They should be told that whatever is said within the group is not reported to anyone's parole officer, supervisor, etc. Notes should not be taken by the group leader. Generally, it is also best to avoid transcriptions such as tape recording. If the leader must use tape recordings, the purpose of these should be for the group to use in playback sessions in order that they may continue discussions about the group and what has occurred. This procedure should be fully explained.

The group leader should be very cautious, especially at the beginning of group sessions, about getting into highly personal matters related to any crime and/or victims of a crime. He might use as a guideline how he would feel if he were an inmate member of the group and was being questioned about his previous behavior. He must control his eagerness to have all inmates participate at an early period. The group leader will have to learn to relax and bring very little or no pressure on persons in the preliminary sessions of the group.

The leader and group members must remember that in the beginning the group is simply a number of individuals getting together with no specific purposes. It is, in fact, a small meeting of inmates. As the leader begins to move the group and the group members become interested in one another, the group takes on special therapeutic qualities. Some members of the group will be indifferent and skeptical, others will be just attentive, and some will be very active. The group leader keeps the group on a constructive plane; and, while the situation is highly unstructured, he keeps the group from wasting time with "chit chat" which is meaningless.

The group leader will have to be willing to modify the continuity of the exchanges in groups according to the atmosphere of the prison. For instance, when unpleasant custodial incidents happen in prison, it may be necessary for the group to spend several days discussing various reactions to these events. At this time, the group leader will be recognized even more as an authority figure and a member of the oppressor group, and suspicions and hostilities among group members may be rampant.

He should relate to inmates that the success of the group will be in accordance with what they are able to give to it. In other words, the inmate should understand that unless he is able to talk about how he feels without undue shame during group sessions, he may not get helpful feedback from the other group members. The inmate must be frank and be able to look at himself and open himself to others; he must face his problems and explain them as he sees them to others as honestly and genuinely as he can. The inmate must understand that one of the basic goals of group counseling or therapy concerns the handling of impulsive behavior—that which leads to criminal acts. He—the inmate—must learn to handle anxiety feelings, inferiority feelings, and various types of hate and hostility feelings, and he must understand that his previous behavior has been extremely costly. He must try to understand why he is in the group—whether he is just trying to get out of prison earlier or whether he wants to be more effectively adjusted once he is outside.

SUMMARY

In the prison setting, the emphasis is most often on incarceration rather than treatment; in fact, the atmosphere may not be supportive of treatment concepts. There is often considerable hostility among the inmates and other employees within the prison. These factors influence the attitudes of inmates not only in the beginning sessions, but throughout therapy sessions. This is why it is particularly important for inmates to understand the purposes and nature of the group work. It is also important for the leader to promise little in terms of results.

Problems often can arise when new inmates enter groups that are ongoing; and, in fact, when there is a substantial turnover, the demise of the group can come about. The turnover also can be used effectively in that, in a sense "new blood" is put into the group as inmates experience on a deeply personal level various new individuals who may wish to sit and listen in their first few sessions and later join in after seeing what advantages have come to older group members through participation. Group leaders should not expect new members of the group to join in too rapidly to the in-depth experience which should be taking place.

The group leader may want to continue his groups indefinitely by allowing persons to drop out and enter, or he may want to bring certain groups to a close according to the feelings of the group members after several sessions. There is no set standard for the number of times the group will meet. In terms of time, two or three hours may be used, or the leader may wish to continue his sessions for six or seven hours. This should be, in effect, decided by members of the group. When groups are of the long-term nature, the leader will gradually learn about individuals in the group. He does not have to spend a great deal of time at the outset in studying case materials; he may learn about the individuals more effectively through interacting with them in the group. The group leader may want to use films or other various materials such as readings, etc., or he may want to simply proceed with interaction among group members.

Role playing can be particularly important and effective with inmates playing the role of the victim, the victim's relative, or the police. There is always a certain awkwardness in beginning role playing. It often carries with it tremendous anxiety feelings for those who are involved. It is certainly worth, however, this amount of unpleasant feeling for all in terms of its end results.

Role playing can become what has been called "psychodrama"—a more complicated and in-depth type of experience which can bring on deeply emotional episodes. The group leader must be particularly effective when this type of in-depth involvement is taking place. The counselor should stay away from this technique unless he has had sufficient training to handle the feelings which may ensue.

As the group continues, some inmates will request individual counseling. This is a good sign that the inmate has real faith in the group leader and the individual counseling should be provided.

SOME BASIC ASSUMPTIONS IN COUNSELING

1. The client has enough freedom to make his own decisions.
2. The counseling session is a special kind of learning situation.
3. Behavior is learned and, therefore, can be changed.
4. The counselor not only recognizes individual differences in his client, but sincerely respects these differences.
5. The total welfare of the client is the counselor's primary consideration in the counseling process.
6. The counselor is sincere in his desire to help his client.
7. The needs of the counselor are fulfilled mostly outside the counseling session and, therefore, are not expressed in the counseling process at the client's expense.
8. The client is willing to assume some of the responsibility for bringing about changes in himself which will result in the kind of person he wants to become.

REFERENCES

Corsini, R.: The theory of change resulting from group therapy. *Group Psychotherapy,* 1951.

Fenton, Norman: *An Introduction to Group Counseling in Correctional Service.* The American Correctional Association, Washington, D. C., 1959.

Gazda, George M.: *Basic Approaches to Group Psychotherapy and Group Counseling.* Springfield, Thomas, 1970.

Gazda, George M., Duncan, J. A., Meadows, M. E.: Counseling and group procedures—report of a survey. *Counselor Education and Supervision,* 305, 1967.

Institute on Rehabilitation Services, *Rehabilitation of the Public Offender, A Training Guide*. U. S. Department of Health, Education and Welfare, Rehabilitation Services Administration, Washington, D.C., 1967.

Stefflre, Buford: *Theories of Counseling*. New York, McGraw-Hill, 1965.

Truax, C.D.: Effective ingredients in psychotherapy: An approach to unraveling the patient-therapist interaction. *Journal of Counseling Psychology,* 1963.

CHAPTER V

THE USE OF TWO GROUP METHODS WITH SEVERELY DISABLED PERSONS*

Joyce Testa Salhoot

Advantages of the Group Method	Group Education
Definitions of Group Counseling and Group Education	Time-limited vs. Open-ended Group
	Summary
Group Counseling	References

T HE GROUP METHODS and techniques used with most client populations can be effectively utilized by the skilled counselor of the severely physically disabled for his clients and their families. In his preparation for a group, the counselor must consider those things which are important to the success of any group. However, in each area of his planning there are certain factors unique to the group counseling of the severely disabled. It is the purpose of this chapter to highlight those unique aspects pertaining to the use of group methods with the severely disabled. This includes the purpose of the group, selection of members, concrete pre-group preparations, leadership, intake, group content and techniques, and a discussion of the time-limited versus the open-ended group concluding the chapter. Although a great deal of education occurs in group counseling a distinction will be made between group counseling and group education. Both have a place in a well-developed rehabilitation program.

*The activities on which this paper has been based have been supported in part by a Research and Training Center Grant (RT-4) from the Social and Rehabilitation Service, Department of Health, Education, and Welfare.

ADVANTAGES OF THE GROUP METHOD

1. For the most part, the severely disabled are the recipients of help and care, seldom having the opportunity to give. This type of deprivation can be destructive over a lifetime (Wright, 1960). Through the interaction process in the group, there is ample opportunity for members to give help and share experiences and feelings, thereby enabling them to enhance their sense of worth. A member who says, "I felt the same way and handled it by . . ." has the opportunity to experience himself as a person with something to offer others.

2. Frequently, physically disabled persons become socially isolated or socially dependent on close family members. The group experience provides a protected situation in which the members can involve themselves in new relationships. They not only broaden their horizons through meeting new people, but, in addition, test their social selves and skills in the development of new relationships. Often this facet of the person has become clumsy from disuse. Many times lasting friendships result or members will go on to form a social organization (Montgomery, 1968).

3. For those persons who are reluctant to express their feelings, the group offers a less intense environment than does individual counseling. Often a silent participant's feelings are expressed by others. Through the group's use of these expressions, he may eventually feel safe in expressing himself. Even those members who remain quiet throughout the sessions can receive help. One-to-one counseling requires that the client take an active role.

4. Another advantage offered by the group method is that some subjects can be dealt with more effectively than in the one-to-one method. Most often the severely disabled are wrestling with similar problems; however, the group brings the richness of differing perspectives and diverse solutions. As counselors of the disabled, most of us have had our clients say, "You couldn't possibly understand, you're walking". This "you're not in my shoes" reaction is at times a rationalization, but even so it serves as a realistic barrier. However, in a group this reaction can be dealt with by members (who are in the "same shoes") responding to each other.

5. The development of communication skills is essential if the physically disabled person is to ultimately make a satisfactory adapta-

tion. His increased reliance on others makes it necessary for him to verbalize his needs clearly and tactfully in order to attain the help he needs and at the same time protect and maintain relationships. Unfortunately, the burden is on the disabled person for initiating new relationships or even conversation with old friends after the onset of the disability. Others look to him for clues. The development of communication skills, the value of which cannot be over-estimated, can be learned and practiced more effectively in a group setting.

DEFINITIONS OF GROUP COUNSELING AND GROUP EDUCATION

The distinctions between group counseling and group education are not always clear since there is also much learning in the former. Group counseling is problem-solving oriented in that the group works on individual problems of the members. It is also assumed that there is broader self-understanding occurring through one's performance in the group as he interacts with other members and with the leader while working on tasks. (Group counseling is distinguished from group therapy which is designed to remove pathological blocks in the personality.)

Group education, on the other hand, through discussion and information giving, aims at examining all sides of issues. There is no pressure for conformity or consensus and no follow-up as to whether persons have put into action their verbal commitment (Auerback, 1968). The important result is that individuals are provided with a better basis for making judgments. This method builds on the personality strengths of individuals. Two outlines of group content using this method are presented later in the chapter.

GROUP COUNSELING

Purpose

Establishing a specific, clear, and reasonable purpose for the formation of the group is the first and perhaps most crucial task of the counselor. Many groups are lost before the first meeting because the *leader* is not clear about the purpose. Other groups are unproductive and lack direction because the *members* of the group do not know their purpose. Purpose must be based on the needs of the clients. Many unnecessary mistakes are made when a group is formed solely because there happens to be several clients available.

More favorably, the formation of a group should be considered when the counselor recognizes that many clients have similar needs which he determines can be met in a group. To re-emphasize, the purpose should be specific and reasonable rather than vague and all inclusive.

Vague Purposes

To improve social functioning
To discuss problems
To explore feelings about the disability
To discuss work
To improve communication

Specific Purposes

To prepare for successful job interviews
To work on those things that make a good worker
To discuss and work on the stresses in the family and the new roles as parents of a child with a disability
To discuss concerns and plans of an upcoming discharge from the hospital
To work on those problems and concerns which are occurring on the job

In any contact the leader has with the clients before the first meeting, the purpose of the group should be discussed. Since the clarity of purpose is so essential, the initial primary task during the first session is to discuss the purpose with the group and make a contract that is agreeable. The contract should also include expectations the leader has of the members and what the clients can expect of the leader.

The purpose of the group often changes as goals are accomplished and new problems uncovered. When the purpose changes, it should again be discussed in the group and a new contract made. For example, the leader may comment, "It seems that in working on your concerns about your disabled children, many difficulties with the marital relationships have been voiced. Is this an area on which the group would like to spend time?"

Selection of Members

As with other counseling groups, there should be enough homogeneity in membership for cohesion and enough heterogeneity to stimulate discussion, some conflict, and differing opinions. The most potent cohesive factor is the similarity of the needs of the members.

A common concern of the leader is whether to mix persons with differing disabilities in the same group. It is wise to remind oneself that the composition of the group must relate to the purpose. If for example, the purpose of a group is to evaluate daily performance in a workshop, the nature of the disability would not be a factor in member selection. However, there are counseling groups in which the discussion and purpose are related to emotional reactions to disability. Here the severity of the disability could be a major factor in the selection. In this kind of group an obstacle may be created through mixing people who are completely dependent, such as quadriplegics, with persons who are independent and who have relatively easy access to the community. It might be quite difficult for example, for a person with a below-the-knee amputation and a person with a high spinal cord lesion to identify with each other. The severity of the physical disabilities should be evaluated in relationship to the purpose of the group. Seldom would it be advisable to place an intellectually impaired person or one with unintelligible speech in a group in which other members are free of these problems. In all likelihood, the atypical member would not receive much help and in addition he may serve as a distraction to the other members.

There are two other major cautions for the counselor of the severely disabled, whether working directly with the disabled clients or their family members. In general, it is not advisable to place a physically disabled person with severe psychiatric problems in a group with those who only have a physical disability. For the person with a psychiatric problem, group psychotherapy may be considered rather than counseling.

Secondly, in a group of the severely disabled it is necessary for the members to be able to consider the possibility that the physical problem is *at least* long-term if not permanent, since goals and plans should be formulated by each individual. Therefore, persons who have a rigid denial system do not benefit from the group and in addition, if included, the leader risks his relationship with the client if the group attacks the defense. The client may reject the counselor along with the "bad news". Those still in the shock phase are not candidates for a group (Fink, 1967).

Size of Group and Length of Sessions

The same factors which govern the size of other counseling groups are valid with the severely disabled. Six to nine members is considered a good size. Because there are numerous factors which may interfere with the disabled members' regular attendance or continuation, it is recommended that the counselor select one or two additional members.

The length of the session will depend on the physical tolerance of the clients, the length of the series, and the setting from which the persons are coming. The most standard length is two hours per session. However, compromises are often necessary, especially if the members are in a hospital or other institution where there is a rigid routine involving other personnel. Consideration must also be given to the amount of time required for the members to assemble. With the severely disabled who need help getting to the session and getting settled in the room, often fifteen minutes must be allowed. It is obvious then that sessions of one and a half hours leave little more than one hour for discussion. Of course, if the sessions are held three or more times a week, one hour may be ample.

Pre-group Preparations

Attention to the logistics discussed in this section is crucial, especially when the group is composed of many persons who are physically dependent and/or institutionalized. If adequate pre-group planning is not done, the leader's energy can be sapped before the group begins dealing with last minute problems.

To highlight the range of things to be checked the following illustration is given. This is a ten session, predischarge group of nine persons with quadriplegia who are in a rehabilitation facility.

1. *Room*—Select a room that is large enough to accommodate nine wheelchairs with some room to spare in the event that a mem-

ber has to come in a bed. Working in a hospital, I have found it preferable to have the person come however he can, whether in bed, on a stryker frame, or on a standing board, rather than miss the group. In the event that a member needs to leave the group early, there should be room enough to wheel him out without having to move several other persons. Where there is limited space, seat anyone anticipating an early departure by the door.

The room should be as informal and comfortable as possible and free from architectual barriers. A table is not necessary or useful for the wheelchair bound except to make the leader more comfortable. Usually it is impossible to assemble around one. The room should be conducive to the members forming a circle so that eye contact is optimized. (Eye contact must sometimes be compromised when a member attends in a position other than sitting.) Generally, it should not be so troublesome for the members (or the staff who must transport) to get to the group that they decide it is not worth the effort.

2. *Written Notification*—Written notification should be sent to all persons or departments affected by the members' change of routine and to those who are to transport them. In a hospital this can amount to twenty-five or more memos. I have found that a primary reason for absenteeism is failure of staff to know about the group and therefore not assist the members to get ready.

3. *Refreshments*—Coffee or other drink can add to the informality and comfort of the group, or it can completely disrupt it. Refreshments are of course no problem if the group members can get them and consume them without assistance. For those persons who have limited hand function, having refreshments requires special planning. If there are persons who can help others, seating may be arranged to facilitate this. The members should be alerted to bring their lapboards for the wheelchair to set the drink on. Straws should also be available.

If each group member requires assistance and the leader attempts to provide it himself, the group can easily become quite disrupted. In this case refreshments should not be served.

4. *Attendant*—With a group of severely disabled who are hospitalized, the counselor must consider the possibility of a group member needing unexpected physical assistance during a meeting. Having an attendant who is on the staff of the institution in the room can be

distracting and can inhibit discussion. The counselor may prefer to have an attendant available outside the room whom he can call.

5. *Priority of Group*—In most medically oriented rehabilitation settings the patients have many unscheduled events, a consulting physician to see, lab work to be done, X-ray, etc. In order to minimize, if not eliminate interruptions, the counselor should have appropriate approval for the patients' participation as well as a clear interpretation from the administration to all the services as to the priority of the group. A group cannot function if the process is continually interrupted by its members being removed. If the group is to have importance to the members and if it is to be effective, it must be given priority while it is in session. Using in-service training to acquaint the staff with the nature of the group and its accomplishments will often promote cooperation.

Leadership

The choice most often is single or co-leadership. The latter is the most popular type especially for beginning group counselors and it does offer several advantages.

1. Co-leaders increase the confidence of each other. Group counseling with the severely disabled is comparable to sailing on uncharted seas. There is little written specifically about it and there seem to be so many obstacles to using traditional group counseling guidelines with this population. Consequently, even trained group leaders may have the tendency to be uneasy, initially.

2. The preparation can be divided and therefore lighten each leader's role.

3. Having eye contact with all members is enhanced by the presence of two leaders when the members are sitting in a circle and lack mobility.

4. Co-leadership provides the essential backup if one leader is absent. Because of the amount of preparation necessary, it would be an imposition on many persons to cancel.

5. Two leaders are able to serve the group as a model for interaction. Through it, members can see good communication skills in action especially if the leaders are free to disagree, compromise, and problem-solve.

6. Group counseling with the severely disabled can be emotionally

very draining. The nature of their problems are often monumental and frequently without adequate solution. With two active leaders to share the responsibility, the experience can be less depleting.

In selecting co-leaders for an all-client group, a man-woman team should be considered. Since the disability often impinges on the person's normal life roles and those of his family, there generally is much conflict with man-woman roles whether they be husband-wife, mother-son, or boyfriend-girlfriend. Having both sexes represented can make it easier to evaluate and work on problems of this nature. If the group is composed of couples, a man-woman team is essential so that each sex feels represented.

Single leadership is the other most popular choice. The counselor who leads a group alone would benefit from having had some previous training and experience in group dynamics or at least having available to the leader supervision from a trained person. An additional advantage for the single leader is to tape record the sessions to evaluate progress of the group and to aid in his own supervision.

Intake

Intake is not always necessary or vital, but it usually helps if it can be done. It will depend on the setting and the purpose of the group. Sometimes the referral procedure will be all that is necessary, for example, all new vocational clients or all persons returning for their first follow-up appointment.

If the counselor can manage to have one short interview with each potential group member, he can screen out those persons who are poor candidates. It also gives the leader an opportunity to assess where each member is in his adaptation process, to explain the purpose of the group, and to assess the physical functioning of the clients. It may provide added comfort to members to meet the leader(s) before the first meeting.

Group Content and Techniques

Through the facilitation of the leader, the phases of the group should develop systematically. As in individual counseling, there is a beginning (testing), a middle (problem-solving), and an end (termination). Extra care should be given in diagnosing the stage in which the group is functioning because of the potentially painful material that the members may share in trying to face the disability. If painful material is revealed too early, that is, before the testing has occurred and trust is established, members may be reluctant to deal with it again when the group is ready to problem-solve. New group leaders in their eagerness are sometimes prone to encourage members to share painful feelings very quickly because they equate this kind of interaction with a successful group. Catharsis is generally not the entire goal in and of itself, although many groups unfortunately never get any further. Problem-solving is the goal and so expressions of feelings should lead to it.

The content of the group will of course be defined by the purpose. Although the members will have many and great concerns in other areas, the group should relate itself to those purposes for which they made a contract. A common defense in groups is avoidance of problem-solving by verbalizing an endless list of problems, all very real. The gravity and number of presented problems can overwhelm the leader; and result in his losing control of the group. For example, in a group in which workshop performance is evaluated, spending a great deal of time on family conflicts is inappropriate. It seems that the totality of the problems experienced by the severely disabled can increase the anxiety of the leader to the extent that he permits the group to attempt working on all problems at once.

A reality oriented approach with focus on the present time is productive. Exclusive focus on pyschodynamics can frustrate members and leads nowhere. This is especially tempting in discussing feelings surrounding dependency, a painful issue. If it is within the purpose of the group, the leader should enable the group to learn new ways to cope with feelings and, when possible, new ways to express independence.

Another common mistake made in groups, especially those held within an institution, is to focus too intensively on the future. The group may attempt to deal with nebulous questions, such as, "How will I feel when I leave?" This future orientation is most fruitless with members who have seldom been out of the rehabilitation center since the onset of the disability. They have no comparable life experience. One technique for dealing with potential future problems is to make them here and now through role playing.

The techniques that may be used in the group are as varied

as is the leader's creativity. In counseling groups, discussion is the primary technique. Productivity can be enhanced by supplementing it with others. Role playing is an excellent method of making a situation real so it can be discussed and felt. In vocational settings, role playing works well in practicing for job interviewing, working on employee and employer or supervisor problems, and problems between employees. Role playing can be used spontaneously at those times during the group when a member is relating a situation which fails to come across clearly to the other members, or when a member is unable to visualize himself in a particular situation.

> A teen-age group of spinal cord injured persons was struggling with the issues of dating. Most could not see themselves approaching someone for a date and all could not fully appreciate the feelings of the other person. The group leaders decided to role play it out on the spot. A male patient played himself asking a girl (the female co-leader) on a date. Half the group was asked to identify with the patient and the other half with the girl. The group members amazed themselves by finding that there could be many reasons for some one to turn down a date, not just the disability. The young man also had practice in saying the words he thought he could not say.

Dividing the group so as to identify with each side of the issue being role played helps the members appreciate both views.

When group sessions are video or audio taped, instant feedback is available to the group. A client who is role playing a job interview may not be aware as to how he is coming across although the other group members provide verbal feedback. In replaying the tape he can identify those areas in which he needs improvement and also he observes those things he is doing well. This technique is used frequently to bring attention to problems, but it is also a potent reinforcement for positive behavior and action.

As previously mentioned, development of communication skills is essential if the physically disabled person is to make a good adaptation. Well-planned use of communication games can be fun and productive. There are games that help members gain insight into the effects of body position, eye contact, presumption of meaning, reactions to criticism and compliments, and general uneasiness in respect to expressing feelings (Satir, 1972). For example, Satir points out clearly that the person with the highest position from the floor has the upper hand. This can be felt quickly if two people try to argue while one is sitting and the other standing. The disabled person frequently finds himself in the less advantageous position. Acting out a situation of this nature in the group can alert the members to possible effects of position on their communication and may lead to the discovery of innovative ways of preventing this from occurring regularly.

Unfortunately, most of us are more experienced in offering criticism than we are in expressing appreciation and other positive feelings. The disabled person needs the ability to express both tactfully. The group can be a vehicle for gaining this experience through games.

> In a group of hospitalized, severely disabled young persons which had met several times, the group learned that one young lady would miss the upcoming three sessions because of major surgery. She had expressed her concern and anxiety about it. In the last minutes of her final session with the group prior to the operation, the leaders expressed how she would be missed and asked each member to tell the girl one thing they appreciated about her. She was instructed only to respond with a "thank you". She stated later that it had a great meaning to her and lessened her anxiety about surgery. The members gained experience in relating positive feelings.

Investigating techniques that may increase communication skills is well worth the counselor's effort. According to Satir, communication is the greatest single factor affecting a person's health and his relationship to others.

There are times in any group when things come to a stand-still. This is a fear of most new leaders, and at such times they feel called upon to do something. With the disabled, this frequently occurs around a painful issue and when members tend to overprotect each other. A useful technique for the leader is to comment on what is happening, the process, rather than forcing the subject.

> In the group Pat expresses her fear that no one will ask her on a date when she leaves the hospital. Others comment, "Don't be silly.", "You will get millions of dates.", etc. Then there is silence. The leader after trying unsuccessfully to enable the group to discuss the real issues says, "What is happening? We can't seem to discuss Pat's concern."

The members bring out that they are trying to keep Pat from worrying, but they share similar concerns in their own lives.

One of the overall purposes of group counseling is to teach the members the problem-solving method so they can implement it as the need arises in their daily lives. This, of course, is not done directly but is a side effect of solving individual problems in the group.

GROUP EDUCATION

Through examining all sides of issues, group education aims at developing a better basis for making judgments. Prevention of problems is an inherent goal. It is an excellent method for clients and families because of the adaptations they are called upon to make in their life roles and the amount of knowledge they will need to maintain the disabled client's state of well being. This method builds on the strengths of members and their capacity to learn by experience.

In using this type of group, the counselor establishes purpose, selects members, determines length of sessions, and makes pre-group preparations with the same guidelines used for group counseling. This kind of group can be much larger than the former, as many as eighteen to twenty-four members. However, there are several special considerations to be pointed out in respect to leadership, the use of other professionals, and content.

Leadership

Knowledge of group dynamics is as essential to the leader of an education group as it is to a counseling group. The word "education" can be misleading in this regard. The leader enables the process to occur and assesses each individual. As members interact in the group, the leader must know what kind of material and action are appropriate for use in this type of group. Lack of sensitivity in this area leads to mixing methods and diluting effectiveness.

In a group which is preparing for first job interviews, John tells how overprotective his mother is and how she deters him from thinking of working. Instead of bringing John back to the subject with a supportive comment, the leader and the group try to analyze the problem and soon the session is lost. As important as family relations are in one's work attitude, it is not appropriate to delve into the subject in this group.

Use of Other Professionals

As the group needs specialized information, other professionals may be brought into the group to provide it. Most will have had no group experience with clients and families and therefore, might be quite anxious. As a result, they may want to lecture rather than engage in an informal discussion, which is usually most productive. They will need to know what the leader is expecting of them and what kind of help the leader will provide during the meeting. They should be cautioned against providing highly scientific information. Instead, practical and useful information is far more helpful.

The individuals from other professions should be selected with care. A knowledgeable yet warm and flexible person who can listen and learn is the best choice. Often they will know the group members and in fact, may have provided service to them on an individual basis. If so, this experience can be an excellent opportunity for the guests to get feedback as to the effectiveness of their services. This kind of experience for professionals gives them a unique chance to gain added insight into the needs of clients and families. (Every person I have used in this capacity expressed astonishment at how much they learned about the real needs of the patients and families.) The leader is instrumental in interpreting questions and answers as well as helping members express their real concerns. The group at all times is the leader's first obligation. Occasionally a situation will occur which will call for implementing this principle.

A nurse was asked to attend a session of patient education for spinal cord injured to discuss home care. The patients had been experiencing some problems on the ward and had pent-up feelings which they began to express by verbally attacking the nurse. Despite efforts of the leader to interpret the meaning so the group could examine it, the nurse began trembling and walked out. The leaders continued with the group in working on the explosive feelings.

Although other professionals are asked to join a group meeting, the leader does not transfer any of his leadership responsibilities to them.

Content

For the most part, the same guidelines and techniques outlined for group counseling are pertinent to this type of group. However, for education, the content may be either unstructured or structured depending on the purpose and needs of the group. In the former the subject matter is derived through discussion. In the latter an agenda is followed, developed by the leader(s) or the leader(s) and the group during the first session. Some flexibility should be built into the agenda to allow for change.

Sample agendas are illustrated in Tables V-I, V-II, and V-III. The first two tables show a two-part program used for hospitalized

TABLE V-I
Sample Program
Patient Education Series*
Phase I
Focus-Hospital

Session	Topic	Leaders
1.	A. Orientation—purpose, method, ground rules B. Discussion of Hospital Life—i.e., patients' rights, privacy, interpersonal problems on ward, organizational structure of hospital in respect to teams.	co-leaders (male and female social workers)
2.	Staff-patient Relationships	co-leaders
3.	Spinal Cord Injury and Its Implications—elementary description of what has happened; frank discussion of prognosis; brief but general information ragarding the skin, bowel, and bladder aspects.	co-leaders and physician
4.	Reactions to Prognosis—adaptations; emotional processes patient and family are going through.	co-leaders
5.	Role and Accomplishments of Physical Therapy—presentation of each patient's muscle test and functional test; activity programing.	co-leaders and physical therapist
6.	Establishment of Problem Solving Process—through discussing specific problems with the hospital staff, family members, and the members' reactions.	co-leaders
7.	Open Discussion of Entire Content of Phase I; Critique	co-leaders

*This program has been used at the Texas Institute for Rehabilitation and Research, Houston, Texas, for spinal cord injured persons.

TABLE V-II
Sample Program
Patient Education Series*
Phase II
Focus-Home

Session	*Topic*	*Leader*
1.	A. Review of Phase I B. Orientation to Phase II—focus on home and community; beginning discussion of concerns related to discharge.	co-leaders
2.	Home Care—adaptation of nursing care to family life; necessary supplies, helpful aids; use and care of equipment; means for improvising to save money.	co-leaders and nurse and O. T.
3.	Adjustments in the Home—possible reactions of patients and families to going home; importance of communication.	co-leaders
4.	Sexual Functioning (males)—a mature verbal ex-patient discussing his experiences (women meet with female leader and a nurse).	male leader ex-patient physician
5.	Role of Work—attitudes of employer, co-worker, college community; specific considerations.	co-leaders vocational counselor
6.	Dialogue with Three Outpatients	co-leaders
7.	The Community—open disccssion of sessions 5 and 6; use of available resources.	co-leaders
8.	Medical Review and Follow-up Recommendations —"What to do if?"	co-leaders physician
9.	Summary and Critique of Phase II	co-leaders

*This program has been used at the Texas Institute for Rehabilitation and Research, Houston, Texas, for spinal cord injured persons.

persons with spinal cord injuries. Phase I occurs after the acute medical stage is over; Phase II is offered to those patients approaching discharge. The parent program (Table V-III) has been used for the family members of the patients nearing discharge and for those whose disabled child is already in the home.

TIME-LIMITED VERSUS OPEN-ENDED GROUP

Another choice to be made by the counselor in preparing for either a counseling or an educational group is whether the group is to be

TABLE V-III
Sample Program
Parent Education Series*

Session	Topic	Leaders
1.	A. Orientation—purpose, method and ground rules B. General Discussion of Problem Areas	leader (social worker)
2.	Spinal Cord Injury and Its Implications	leader and physician
3.	Urological Problems (of great concern)	leader and physician
4.	Adaptation of Nursing Care to the Home	leader and nurse
5.	Purpose of Physical Therapy—muscle tests of each parent's patient are reviewed	leader and physical therapist
6.	Sexual Functioning of Spinal Cord Injured Individuals	leader and physician
7.	Educational and Vocational Possibilities	leader and vocational counselor
8.	Patient's relationship to parents and ways in which parents can help patients in assuming independence.	leader
9.	Marital relationship of parents; responsibility toward each other and toward the patient.	leader
10.	Problems with patients' siblings; with interested relatives outside the home.	leader

*This program has been used at the Texas Institute for Rehabilitation and Research, Houston, Texas, for parents of spinal cord injured persons.

time-limited or open-ended. A time-limited group is one in which there is a designated number of sessions, a beginning and ending date, and closed membership, that is, additional members are not routinely added to the group after it is underway. An open-ended group is one in which there is a beginning date but no ending date, and the membership changes. Members terminate and others are added as a matter of course. For example, a pre-discharge group is held twice a week as a regular part of the rehabilitation program. As patients are near discharge, they are added to the group. The group goes on as the membership changes.

The time-limited group is the easiest to plan for and to lead. Because it requires a specific time commitment, the clients find it more convenient. The leader should give consideration to several factors when choosing to do an open-ended group.

1. There should be specific criteria for determining when a person is a candidate for the group and when he is ready for termination.

2. There is a tendency for members to continue coming to the group until they are bored and lose motivation.

3. With the changing membership, the counselor will find persons in various stages of the group process. While some members are in the beginning stage of testing, others will be problem-solving, and some will be in the termination phase. This calls for the leader's making precise individual diagnoses as well as establishing specific goals for each member.

4. Establishing an open-ended group in an institutional setting can have a great impact on the daily routine of other personnel as permanent changes in their work schedules may be necessary to make time for the group to meet. As a result, the leader may find he must do a great deal of interpretation and planning for the group to be accepted by the staff and to get it under way.

It is evident that the open-ended counseling and unstructured educational group require a great deal of skill on the part of the leader. A structured educational group in which the content is repeated can be led quite effectively by a beginning group leader.

SUMMARY

Each of the group methods discussed have a place in a well-developed rehabilitation program for persons with a severe disability and their families. Group counseling, which is problem-solving oriented, is used to help members deal with their individual concerns, thereby learning the problem-solving method. Group education aims at providing members with information and examining all sides of issues so they can make better judgments.

In each phase of his group planning for severely disabled persons and their families, the counselor must give attention to those factors unique to this population. With these factors in mind, the two methods can be quite effective if the leader establishes a specific purpose, makes a contract with the group members, does adequate screening of group candidates, and makes the necessary pre-group preparations.

REFERENCES

Auerback, A. B.: *Parents Learn Through Discussion: Principles and Practices of Parent Group Education.* New York, John Wiley and Sons, 1968.

Fink, S. L.: Crisis and motivation: A theoretical model. *Archives of Physical Medicine and Rehabilitation,* 48:592-597, 1967.

Montgomery, H.: The amandus club. *Nursing Times,* 64:1562-6, 1968.

Owen, S. M.: Is group counseling neglected? *Journal of Rehabilitation,* 38: 12-15, 1972.

Satir, V.: *Peoplemaking.* Palo Alto, Science and Behavior Books, 1972.

Wright, B. A.: *Physical Disability—A Psychological Approach.* New York, Harper and Row, 1960.

CHAPTER VI

MARITAL COUNSELING IN GROUPS

JOHN G. CULL AND RICHARD E. HARDY

Roles in Marital Group
  Settings
Some Procedures
Selection of Group
  Participants
Relationships Necessary for
  Effective Group
  Interaction

Modeling Behavior
Problems Which May
  Surface During Group
  Marital Counseling
Ground Rules for Group
  Marital Sessions
Time Periods and Types of
  Sessions

ROLES IN MARITAL GROUP SETTINGS

OFTEN IN COUNSELING, it is difficult to discriminate between actual behavior (role played) and behavior which is related by a marriage partner. This period of counseling is difficult. The marriage counselor is interacting on a one-to-one basis or is occasionally seeing both marriage partners together. As a result of the defensiveness and ego protective behavior of the individual, quite often there is a great degree of uncertainty as to the reality of the roles which are being reported. When it is evident that there is a reality base for some of the reports of an antagonistic spouse, the question remains concerning the impact of this role, the substance of the role, and its prevalence. When a marriage starts deteriorating, it is quite natural for each partner to try to justify his position and to displace blame and responsibility for the deterioration of the marriage through recriminations and the imputing of negative roles on the other partner.

Group work is an ideal approach to be used in separating these diverse roles which are so basic in the marital interaction. As the therapist observes the individuals and their role within the group, he can make a direct connection between the role an individual adopts in

99

the group setting and the role he tends to play most often in the marital setting. In individual counseling the client may appear somewhat passive, withdrawn, taciturn, and relate his reaction to others and events in a philosophical manner; however, in group interactions, it is quite possible for him to change drastically and become the aggressor rather than the passive receptor in a relationship.

The Aggressive Individual

As an aggressor he may work in many ways to exert his will. He may be oblivious or unconcerned about the feelings of others. He will override their concerns by deflating them, attempting to relegate them to a lower status, either expressing disapproval or ignoring their feelings, their value system, or the acts in which they engage and which are counter to his basic goals. He will appear to be highly goal-oriented regardless of the cost in achieving that goal, and he will work toward the goal regardless of the hurt feelings and the inner damage to his interpersonal relationships. He works toward the goal which he perceives as the one bringing him the most recognition. Under this set of circumstances, this individual will be most manipulative in that he will show the highest degree of Machiavellianism. He will be somewhat jealous of individuals who gain more recognition than he does and he will be sympathetic toward the individuals whom he outshines most readily.

The Acceptance Seeker

Related to the individual who has a high degree of need to accomplish the goals he perceives as important and who accomplishes them through aggressive-type behavior is the individual whose concern is not the accomplishment of the goals, but whose goal is to receive acceptance by the group or one who feels the need for recognition within the group. This is an individual who is quite insecure and tends to need almost continual positive reinforcement as to his self-adequacy and his value to the group or to the marriage partner. This type of individual demonstrates his needs in the group in many ways. Generally, he will not be as oriented toward the goal which is perceived by the group as the group goal as will be the aggressive-type individual, but he will work toward the goal if he feels it will bring a great deal of recognition. Much of his overt behavior upon examination will be seen to be self-serving and self-gratifying behavior rather than goal-oriented behavior. It has been our experience in group work with marriage partners that this type of individual has many more needs than the aggressive-type individual. If the individual who is seeking the recognition to the exclusion of everything else has a spouse who attempts to meet these needs, quite often the needs are so great the spouse loses the impact she once had to fulfill his needs; therefore, he looks elsewhere for the recognition which is so essential to his personality integration. He responds to her as being unconcerned about him, as not really understanding his motivations, and gives the impression that the spouse is somewhat self-centered and uncooperative in the marriage pact. In the group situation, the individual demonstrates his need for recognition by behavior and mannerisms both verbal and nonverbal which call attention to himself. He will quite often boast; he will feel the need to relate personal experiences; he will relate his accomplishments and achievements; perhaps he may relate them in a thinly veiled manner under the guise of using them as an example to make a point in some other area; however, he feels compelled to bring forth his accomplishments, his values, his attributes to the group and to hold them out for group approval. His most painful moments in the group will be when he perceives he has been devalued by other members in the group and placed in an inferior position or when he feels he is demonstrating behavior which is characterized by the group as inadequacy.

The Sympathy Seeker

On a continuum down from the aggressive-type individual to the individual who is seeking recognition from the group, is the next type of personality which may be characterized as the sympathy seeker. This individual attempts to elicit responses of sympathy from the group thereby obviating any pressures for him to achieve either within the group or without the group. As he depreciates himself and relegates himself to a lower inferior position, he gets the sympathy of the group and at the same time is absolved of responsibility within the group. This provides him a haven of irresponsibility. He is able to go his own way; he can follow the group or he can elect to remain aloof from the group—all with the approval of the group as a result of his being in a position to receive sympathy from the group. As the group becomes more demanding and insistent on his contributing, he will reinforce his protestations of inferiority, illness, of devaluation, or of a generalized inadequacy. He will attempt to reinforce the group's feelings of sympathy for him in order to free himself from entanglements of the group. If he is unsuccessful in his attempts to get sympathy from the group, he will attempt to split the group into smaller units and will see statements of sympathy from the smaller subgroups. The value of the group interaction is to denote how an individual who is a sympathy seeker behaves in the group setting; but in the marriage relationship and when seen on an individual counseling basis may come through as a relatively independent sort of person who expresses feelings of adequacy and concern for the marriage relationship. The group setting will highlight the change when his behavior is observed and the pressures of the group are exerted.

The Confessor

The next type of behavior which is brought out in a group is confessing behavior. This is behavior that is characterized by rather superficial confessing. As the individual sees that the demands are getting greater to reveal himself and as he sees that his responsibility will have to be fulfilled if he is to maintain membership in the group, quite often he starts confessing in a very superficial manner to the group. Generally, confessions are characterized by large quantity and low quality information the confessor feels that the more he confesses, the more he absolves himself of responsibility for honest group interaction. He confesses to his feelings which are somewhat insignificant in a very sober, concerned fashion. He professes to have immediate insight as a result of the group sessions. When an individual starts to criticize him, this confessing-type individual immediately stifles the criticism or comments by agreeing with the critic and going even further in confessing these feelings or attributes related to these on and on *ad nauseam*.

In a marriage, this is a very effective defense. It's quite frustrating when the marriage partner tries to communicate and is thwarted through this self-confessing type behavior. Communication is effectively blocked when one marriage partner takes the ball and runs by this superficial type of confessing behavior. When this type of behavior is exhibited, it is quite difficult to get to the core of the problem in individual counseling since the confessor is verbalizing a great deal of concern, flexibility, and willingness to cooperate when in fact his behavior is aimed more at stifling communication and blocking effective understandings within the marriage relationship.

The Externalizer

Another type of behavior which is exhibited in groups can be characterized by the term "externalization". The externalizer is an individual who becomes uncomfortable in the interaction and the "give and take" which is occurring in the group or which occurs in close interpersonal relationships; therefore, in order to escape from the impact of these interpersonal relationships, he tends to focus on problems that are external to the group or external to the relationship. As the group starts to focus on the individual or as the group gets too close to the individual, he starts externalizing in order to shift the brunt of an attack or the brunt of an inquisition from him on to some external object. Quite often this can be a very effective maneuver; however, it is one which is highly frustrating to an individal who is seriously trying to resolve conflicts. An effective externalizer is able to communicate his values, his impressions, his attitudes and beliefs very effectively without referring to himself. He does this through injecting or projecting his attitudes into the attitudes of groups external to the interaction in which he is currently engaged. Consequently, he is able to communicate a point of view which he holds without allowing others to adequately communicate their points of view.

The Isolate

The next type of behavior which is observed in the group setting and has a direct referent back to marital interactions is that of the isolate. This is the behavior of the individual who decides to insulate himself from the interaction of the group. He very definitely elects not to interact with the group and decides to disallow the group from interacting with him. He quite often will make a very studied effort to inform the group of his nonchalance, of his decision to be noninvolved. He does this quite often by engaging in strategems which are distracting to the group but give no indication of his interest or willingness to contribute to the group. He may attract the attention of one or two other members of the group and start to play with them. He may become very animated in doodling. He may develop little games which he plays with himself such as folding paper, making airplanes, drawing pictures of the room. When confronted, his general response is, "I'm paying attention", "I'm listening", "I'm participating", "I just engage in these little activities to heighten my sensitivity to what's going on". This individual generally will not allow himself to be drawn into the interaction within the group. He will stay outside the mainstream of activity and will attempt to communicate his intentions through nonverbal behavior. His verbal behavior will be one of conciliation and concern.

The Dominator

The next type of behavior on the continuum from highly goal-oriented to highly negativistic will be that of the individual who tries to dominate one or more individuals in the group or tries to dominate the entire group. His drives toward domination are an effort to convince others of his authority and superiority. His interests are not as goal-oriented as the aggressive-type individual who sacrifices others' feelings and his own interpersonal relationship with others in an effort to accomplish a group goal; however, the dominating-type individual is concerned with exerting influence over others not for the goal which can be achieved but just for the sake of dominance. If there is a highly aggressive individual in the group and also a dominating individual in the group, the more maladaptive type of behavior will be exhibited by the dominating individual for he will find the need to express his adequacy by wooing group members away from the goal-oriented aggressive-type individual whose drives are to move the group toward a goal. The dominator will achieve his purpose if he subverts the actions or intents of the aggressive individual. The dominating individual is concerned with achieving a status of respect. He may do this through many types of behavior such as being punitive and using the threat of punitive behavior to tower a weaker member. He may use flattery to woo a group member. He may use the power of suggestion and persuasion or he may just attempt to verbally and socially overpower the other individuals to force them into submission. In a marriage relationship, this type individual most often has to have a wife who is somewhat passive and one who does not have a high level of need for individuality and expressions of self-adequacy through the approval of their spouse.

The Antagonist

The next and last type of behavior to be discussed is that of the antagonist. This is the individual who strives for self-adequacy and recognition through the negativistic behavior and values he adopts. He is somewhat arbitrary and capricious in his value judgments. The underlying constant of his judgments is the contrariness of his position. He seems to be at odds with the mainstream of opinion, values, or actions within the group interaction. His negativism can be quite harsh and sharp. He apparently is unconcerned about the feelings of others in the group. The most important thing to him is to exhibit his individuality by disagreeing with the group consensus. He is stubbornly resistent to coercion or persuasion. He will go so far as to disrupt the flow of the work of the group by attempting to change directions, change the topic of concern, alter the goal which the group is working toward, or try to redefine the ground rules which were established in the group. He takes a negative view of life and is antagonistic to almost all of the members in the group. He is argumentative and can be quite bombastic when thwarted.

In marital counseling, it is essential to see the clients in an individual, one-to-one situation. It is equally important to see spouses together; however, we feel that it is of utmost importance for effective marriage counseling to supplement individual counseling with group techniques, for it is through group techniques that much of the behavior which can remain enigmatic in individual counseling is delineated and exemplified by pressures and interactions of the group. Much of the behavior which has constituted irritant influences to the marriage pact is elicited in the group situation. This type of behavior is on the surface in the group. It can be observed by the therapist, and in the individual sessions which follow, it can be related to the individual and interpreted for him to review and evaluate and react to. Without the benefit of the group, marital counseling is much slower and a much longer process. Many times, marriage will continue to deteriorate at a faster rate than the therapist is able to diagnose and treat the irritants which are precipitating the deterioration.

SOME PROCEDURES

There is an exercise in group behavior which requires working toward the solution of a problem concerned with being marooned on the moon. The problem requires individuals to react by rank ordering a number of various types of equipment which they would choose to have with them if they were so marooned. The exercise which has been checked by space experts at the National Space and Aeronautics Administration is first completed by individuals and later by a group of six to eight persons working togther. The usual result of the exercise is that group behavior is demonstrated over and over again to be more effective in getting at correct solutions to problems than is individual effort alone. In some few cases the individual's decision may be more effective than that of the group, but in most cases the group decision is more nearly correct than the individual one.

The purpose of the exercise is to demonstrate the effectiveness of group interaction in problem solving. Just as the exercise does demonstrate the effectiveness of increased interaction among individuals in problem solving, so does group marital counseling achieve much more in many cases than does the basic interaction between the client and therapist. While much can be accomplished by individual sessions with the client, it is our feeling that supplemental group sessions can bring about enormous strides in understanding and adjustment.

SELECTION OF GROUP PARTICIPANTS

In group marital counseling, one generally has a decision to make concerning whether he wants to have in his group only husbands, only wives, or mix the group. He also needs to make a decision whether husbands and wives will be in the same group. When husband and wife are in the same group, other members of the group can help them explore in considerable detail their problem areas. When husband or wives are in groups made up exclusively of all males or all females, the group leader will experience some difficulty in keeping the session from turning into a complaint session about the opposite sex. When husbands and wives are in groups separately from one another, group members have been shown to be very eager to help the individual to explore his marital situation and understand it more fully. The best combination seems to be one in which both husband and wife are in the same group or husband or wife are in mixed groups of males and females. Heterogeneity has a great affect upon the effectiveness in group interaction and problem solving. Diversity brings with it a certain breath of experience and increases the strength of the group to solve both individual problems and group problems. There is no reason why persons from all walks of life cannot be mixed in a heterogeneous marital group counseling situation. This same opinion would extend to persons of various ages and socio-economic backgrounds.

RELATIONSHIPS NECESSARY FOR EFFECTIVE GROUP INTERACTION

Some of the necessary ingredients for effective group problem exploration include acceptance of others, awareness, self acceptance of individuals in the group, and problem centering approaches to behavior. When these conditions exist, a high "trust" level has been achieved. People are free to be themselves when a level of trust has been established in the group. When the trust level has not been established or is low, group members tend to be manipulative, to hold back information about themselves, and to be defensive. When individuals within the group trust one another, defensiveness is reduced, information flow is multiplied, and the strategies of manipulation are dissipated.

The group leader must create in members a feeling of freedom. Members can be most valuable as group members, to others in groups, and to themselves when they are free and able to be themselves

MODELING BEHAVIOR

It is the responsibility of the group leader to model the types of behavior which he would like to see exhibited by the various members of the group. The group facilitator or leader should not be overbearing and should not be dominating as a leader but should move the group toward understanding of problems through various behaviors which he not only demonstrates, but models. The group leader should be an individual who is friendly, warm, and accepting. He should be a person who works with others and does not practice techniques upon them. The word "with" suggests that the procedure taking place is a relationship and not a technique oriented process. The atmosphere within the group should be productive of or conducive to good mental and social-psychological health. The goal of all group work is that of the obtainment of good mental health.

Every member of the group should be accorded enough consideration and respect by the group in order that he has at least a modicum
of self-esteem. The individual must be willing and able to accept
himself within a group setting. He must feel that he has the respect
of others and that he is a person of worth. The group environment
should facilitate the development and maintenance of self-esteem.

Members of the group should show considerable acceptance of
others and their attitudes regardless of whether or not group members agree with the attitudes or ideas which are being expressed. In
other words, group members do not have to agree with the ideas
in order to accept them as legitimate personal feelings of the individual expressing them. At times, the needs of individuals in the
group for self-esteem may interfere with their accepting and respecting
others. It has been shown many times that we may want to feel
superior to others, and we do this by bolstering ourselves. When this
is the case, often the person involved does not have enough respect
for himself, therefore, he cannot respect others. Listening to another
is the simplest and one of the most basic ways through which we
can show respect for him.

Group members need to show understanding of other's feelings
and the group leader should demonstrate that he understands how
others feel an that he wishes to get to know them better. If the group
leader uses psychological terminology glibly, he may "turn off" the
group. He should not attempt to demonstrate understanding through
such use of professional jargon, but he should demonstrate that he
has what has been called "accurate empathy" in reference to the
individual. He can put himself in the other's place and understand
feelings as the other person experiences them.

All members of the group must demonstrate some degree of confidence in the other persons in the group. There must be recognition
of the rights and privileges and freedoms to action of others. The
group must be characterized by sincerity, integrity, openness, and
honesty if it is to achieve its goals. These characteristics help eliminate
the threat and help to create an environment in which the individual
can develop to his fullest potential by exploring all aspects of his
particular marital problem. The group leader should give his attention, respect, understanding, and interest to those within the group
who are attempting to work toward a solution of their problems and
help others in doing likewise.

Artificiality must be avoided on the part of the group leader at all costs. There is no real alternative to genuineness in the group counseling process.

The group leader must demonstrate the types of behavior which participants in the group need to exhibit if problem-solving is to take place. There must be a certain amount of risk taking—in other words, individuals in the group must go beyond what is known to be factual in order to explore their behavior. Persons must be willing to do more than to play it safe. If, for instance, within a session an individual becomes angry or anxious, these behaviors can make him appear foolish, but these may be necessary behaviors and necessary risks to take in order for him to achieve success in problem solving. There must be substantial support for others as members attempt to reach goals that are important. Persons can say in various ways that they may not be sure what an individual is aiming toward or proposing, but they support the efforts being made to get something moving or to make others understand a particular problem.

There should be a demonstration that persons are free and able to be open about their feelings and thoughts, and there should be a problem centering or focusing on problems faced by a group rather than on control or method. Problem centering is based upon the assumption that the group can accomplish much more when individuals in groups learn how to solve problems rather than by the leader having to employ certain technique patterns in order to achieve goals. Group members should clearly recognize the feelings of others and how one's feelings are inter-influencing the behavior of others.

Another characteristic which is most important in achieving the level of problem solving ability necessary for success is that of the individual feeling that he can accept his own emotions without denying them or giving rationalizations or apologies. Such acceptance can be evidenced by such statements "I am disgusted or bored with myself because I feel ineffective."

PROBLEMS WHICH MAY SURFACE DURING GROUP MARITAL COUNSELING

There is no beginning or end to the types of human situations which may come to light during marital counseling. Group marital counseling, just as individual counseling and other group counseling, covers the whole realm of human life and experience. Of course, there are sex problems which include frigidity, sterility, impotence, and others. There are the problems of children; there are the problems of incongruencies in expectations, of differences in opinion concerning careers; there is the problem of extramarital affairs, of changing life style in a rapidly moving society, of parents and in-laws and their influence in the marriage. There are identification problems, problems of personal values, the different meanings of love and substitutes for it which are meaningful to some people and not meaningful to others, the expression and management of feelings, the handling of various financial crises, and many others.

The counselor concerned with group marital counseling must be a mature individual who is able to facilitate human learning through the demonstration of the behaviors described earlier. He must know group interactions well and thoroughly understand human behavior.

GROUND RULES FOR GROUP MARITAL SESSIONS

Human interaction includes two major properties: (1) content and (2) process. Content has to do with the subject matter with which the group is concerned. Process has to do with the actual procedure of what is happening between and to group members while the group is working. The group leader must be sensitive to the group process in order to help the group in diagnosing special problems so that these can be dealt with soon and effectively.

One of the important concepts in group interaction is that everyone who is in the group belongs there because he simply is there. This concept is one of the most important ones in effecting successful group behavior. If an individual feels anger toward another person, his behavior does not change his belonging in the group. If a person reads himself out of a group, it does not change his belonging in it. If he gives up on himself, the group does not give up on him.

Each person determines what is true for him by what is in him. Whatever he feels makes sense in himself and whatever way he wishes to live inside himself is determined by what is in him as an individual. Most people live mostly inside themselves. No one knows more about how a person really is than the person himself. The group leader should remember that he should force no one to be more honest than he wants to be just at the moment he is speaking. We should listen for the person who is inside the individual who is living and feeling. This person may not be totally exposed to us at any given time although he may wish to be exposed.

The group leader is always responsible for protecting the "belongingness" of every member to group and also their right to be heard. He is also responsible for the confidential aspect of the group disclosures, which means that no one will repeat anything which has been said outside the group unless it concerns only himself.

Everyone should participate in the group. One indication of involvement is verbal participation. The group leader should look for differences in terms of who are the high and low participators. What are the shifts in participation? How are the persons who are not participating being treated by the others? What subgroups are there? Who keeps the group moving? Which of the groups are high in terms of influence? Are there autocrats and peacemakers? Are there members getting attention by their apparent lack of involvment in the group? Who attempts to include everyone in group discussion decision making? In other words, what are the styles of influence? Is the group drifting from topic to topic? Is this a defensive type of behavior? Do they attempt to become overly organized at the expense of the losing effectiveness in problem solving? Are there persons outside the group?

Is the group avoiding certain topics and setting certain norms for behavior? Is religion or sex avoided, for instance, as a topic? Are the group members being overly nice to each other? Are they agreeing too soon, in short are they avoiding facing individual and group problems?

One of the helpful techniques which can be used in group marital counseling is that of spontaneous role playing. This can be done by husband and wife actually sitting in the center of the group and playing out a particular problematic situation. The group members can then react to various aspects of the role playing and make suggestions in order that the individuals may develop fuller understanding of the problem area. It may also be useful to have a surrogate wife or husband role play with an actual husband and wife.

Role reversal is another technique in which individuals reverse their roles and then role play actual situations. This technique can be most interesting in that the husband plays the wife's part and wife plays the husband's part. It is sometimes easy to bring about understanding through the use of this technique. Persons can relive past events or project future occurrences through role playing.

Another technique which is useful is that of repeating the client's key words or statements. This is particularly useful in terms of what has been called *free association*. In other words, that process of using clues or cues to help the client give meaningful information about himself and his problems.

The group leader should keep in mind that persons who live many psychosomatic complaints may be disguising personal problems and conflicts. He should also remember that the individual group member who offers any complaints about his spouse may be covering his own personal anxieties and inadequacies.

TIME PERIODS AND TYPES OF SESSIONS

The purpose of this chapter has been to describe group marital counseling. Generally, sessions may last for three to four hours and may be ongoing meeting eight to ten more times. This varies from the individual counseling sessions which usually last from 50 to 60 minutes.

Much of the material given in this chapter concerns the facilitating of groups rather than the actual leading of them as a group therapist. It is felt by the authors that selected encounter group concepts can be of substantial benefit in various types of marital counseling.

Of course, it may be that group members will wish to engage in a type of marathon encounter in which they may continue their group activities for 20-24 hours. These sessions can later be followed by shorter two to three hour group sessions for those who are interested. Group leaders should not become discouraged if some of their group members do not choose to return to later group meetings. People vary enormously in their abilities to withstand various types of stress, and many people feel a good deal of insecurity and stress during group counseling work even though substantial efforts have been made to establish an atmosphere of warmth and trust. Some people are able to gain a great deal in a short period of time, and for these persons individual counseling may be more in accordance with their needs than group experiences.

The group counselor, leader or facilitator—whichever name is chosen—must keep in mind that the purpose of the group session is whatever goal the group decides upon. At times a group session may provide real service in terms of being informational in nature. One of the basic problems related to problems in marriage is the preparation for simply living with another person. At times the counselor will find it necessary to assume the role of information giver and tutor in individual sessions, and in group sessions members may find it necessary to be informational in order to achieve basic goals which have been established. Group members can greatly help individuals in the group by exploring the needs of each person. In many cases needs are not being met due to the fact that these needs are not understood by the spouse and often the person himself.

CHAPTER VII

BEHAVIORAL GROUP THERAPY WITH ALCOHOL ABUSERS

STEVEN M. ROSS

Techniques and
    Terminology
Pre-group Preparations

Group Meetings
Conclusion
References

T HIS CHAPTER IS AN attempt to present a broad spectrum behavior approach to group treatment of alcoholism. The emphasis
will be on practical techniques which the reader can use regardless
of his theoretical orientation. Theory, technical vocabulary, and academic arguments will be kept to a minimum, while references will
be provided the reader to obtain more detailed information of various
techniques, the research literature, and other sources.

The approach to be described is based on the assumption that
alcohol abuse is a learning problem in that patients learn to either
escape or avoid unpleasant events or gain access to pleasurable events
through excessive drinking.

If patients learn to respond in these ways to various life events,
it is possible to teach them to respond in ways other than drinking.
The task of the group is to provide a setting where other behaviors
can be learned, practiced, and strengthened. Unless there is more to
be gained by not drinking than by doing so, drinking will persist.
The group must, therefore, also help in generalizing the behaviors
learned in the group to situations where they are most needed outside
the group, namely, in the community.

The group has special advantages for accomplishing these very
difficult tasks, advantages which individual therapy lacks: (1) members are able to learn from each other via observation and imitation,
(2) members learn that their problems are not unique and they are

not alone, (3) new behavior can be practiced and strengthened in the presence of a variety of people which more closely approximates "real life", (4) group censure and support can exert more pressure to bear for change and strengthening of new behaviors, (5) patients learn that they are able to trust and help others, (6) more efficient use of the leader's time is made, and (7) more facets of problems and more problem solving techniques can be gained from group discussion.

Naturally, the total treatment of the alcoholic cannot occur in one therapy group. There are often medical, vocational, and recreational problems which must be left to other members of the treatment team. Oftentimes individuals must be prepared to function in a group, and this preparation itself may take the form of one-to-one counseling or therapy. The leader must decide with each potential group member which problems should be brought up in group and which are better dealt with elsewhere. The key to this problem lies in pre-group preparations, namely, deciding on the kind of group (composition, goals, commonalities of members, time limitations, size) and the assessment of prospective members (identifying behavioral assets, deficits, excesses).

In the sections to follow we will examine these pre-group functions in greater detail, but first it may be helpful to define a few terms which will be used, trying, of course, to adhere to my original promise of keeping technical vacabulary to a minimum. It is more the purpose of this section to provide the reader with a "cookbook" of techniques which he can draw upon regardless of the type of group he runs, than it is to teach a foreign academic language.

TECHNIQUES AND TERMINOLOGY

Baseline rate

This term refers to the frequency, duration, or magnitude with which a particular behavior occurs naturally before any type of treatment takes place. Obtaining baseline rates before treatment provides us with some indication of how successful our treatment is, providing we continue to get data on the same behavior in the same way after treatment begins and ends. If someone drinks a fifth of scotch every day prior to treatment, their baseline drinking rate would be a fifth per day (magnitude). Another way of measuring pre-treatment drinking behavior might be to observe how frequently a patient pours a drink during a particular time sample. The third possibility, duration, might be determined by measuring with a stop watch how many total minutes during a time sample the patient had a drink poured for himself.

It is not necessary to obtain all three measures on any given behavior. For any given behavior whether it be drinking, talking about family problems in a group, or number of A.A. meetings attended, there is usually one best measure to get. A general rule of thumb is if a behavior occurs frequently and lasts only a few seconds, e.g., fidgeting, eye contact, using a particular word, it is probably better to measure frequency of response. If the behavior occurs for several hours or minutes, e.g., tardy for group, feeling depressed, talking in group, it is probably better to measure duration of occurrence per session, per day, etc. Magnitude is probably best used when the behavior already is in some quantified form, e.g., number of ounces of wine consumed in a day or week, how fearful someone rates themself on a scale from 0 to 100. A much more detailed description of data collecting is provided by Jackson and Della-Piana (1972).

While it is not always feasible to obtain baseline rates and subsequent data on all problem behaviors for all patients because of practical limitations of time, personnel, cost, etc., it is possible to a greater degree than one might imagine, especially in a hospital or clinic or through home visits. At the very least, patients themselves can obtain data on their own behavior even if it is something as gross as counting empty bottles. In addition, many friends, family members, employers, and relatives are willing to help as collateral sources of data and general functioning. By comparing several baseline rates we can determine how reliable the measure is, providing the two observers did their data collecting independently of each other. The help of collaterals should never be enlisted without the full knowledge and consent of the patient lest his trust in the treatment program be undermined.

Functional analysis

A functional analysis of behavior is an assessment of what cues set the stage for certain responses to occur and what happens immediately after the responses have occurred which strengthen (reinforce) them or weaken them. All of the behavior we emit which has some effect on ourselves or our environment is controlled by that effect. To change this behavior we must change the effect it has, or we must practice new responses to the old cues. These notions are worth pondering for a few minutes because they are very important but very difficult to achieve.

Consider an individual who claims that he does not know why he drinks. He even says that if he knew why he drank he would not be asking for our help. It is very likely that this individual is telling the truth. He may be unaware of many events that lead to drinking and what the drinking "does for him". If he were to keep records of his drinking, including: What Occurred Just Prior to Drinking, the Date, Time, Place, Alone or Whom With, Amount Consumed, Type of Beverage, What Happened After Drinking, very definite patterns would emerge which would yield much information as to what cues the drinking and what functions the drinking serves. I have had copies of the above information made which I give to people seeking treatment and individiuals they list as collateral sources of information. I call these data sheets the *Intake Record* and often require waiting list patients to complete them in order to qualify for treatment when a vacancy arises. This does not mean that if they have already stopped drinking they must start again to provied pre-treatment baseline data. However, if they do drink or even have an *urge* to drink they are to record the information as accurately as they can.

The patterns which emerge from intake data of this type are often very informative and can be very helpful in setting goals and generating group discussion. For example, an individual reports coming home from work tense and needing a drink to "unwind". Upon arriving home, he finds his wife yelling at the kids and asking him to punish them for misbehavior. This may further upset him because he may not want to punish them for something that happened hours earlier and did not even involve him. Instead of having one drink he may have three. Instead of having the drinks *with* his wife and kids while chatting about the events of the day, he may take the bottle to a secluded location of the house in order to escape the battle. His wife may then turn on him for shirking his responsibilities which results in another three drinks to drown her voice. By now dinner is ready but he is in no mood to eat and has a few more. He and his wife may sleep separately that night. He probably wakes up with a hangover (late because the alarm clock is in the master bedroom and he slept on the couch). Feeling terrible, he has a few to get him going and to give him courage to face the boss who is angry because he is late. At work people look at him twice because he is disheveled. He feels they are staring at him and talking behind his back. His job may be in danger which adds to the pressure he feels he is under. He may try to be a model employee and perform perfectly that day. If he makes a mistake he becomes extremely upset with himself. At lunch he "has a few to steady his nerves".

This individual may be starting a binge or he may be in the middle of one. We could go on to describe the rest of his day but let us stop at this point and look at a functional analysis of his behavior. His Intake Record shows that he first reported an urge to drink upon arriving home in order to unwind. There are two possibilities at this point. Does arriving home *itself* function as a cue for drinking or does the feeling of needing to unwind? Perhaps both do. Careful inspection of his intake pattern might reveal that he automatically drinks whenever he arrives home regardless of how he is feeling and regardless of how well he and his family are getting along. Perhaps he has learned to drink upon arriving home because so much of the time his wife had a drink waiting for him or because the family squabbling made arriving home an aversive event. Pre-group discussion might focus on these possibilities, what else he might do instead of drink, how the group might be of assistance if he brings the problem up in group, and the fact that other group members can be expected to ask for his help for similar kinds of problems.

The second urge to drink or actual drinking that he probably reported on his Intake Record was that additional drinking which occurred after his wife accused him of shirking his responsibilities. Again, inspection of his Intake Record over time might reveal that he almost always drinks after being criticized. Furthermore, the criticism-drinking association is not limited to his wife. The pattern may also reveal that even when his own children criticize him, not to mention his boss, co-workers, and friends, he drinks or has a strong urge to drink. Criticism, then, may also function as a cue for drinking, and he may not even be aware of it. The drinking which follows criticism may enable him to calm down and forget the criticism which had been bothering him. In addition, the drinking may give him courage to tell the criticizer to shut up. The section of the Intake Record which asks, What Happened After Drinking? might, in fact, support these hypotheses by showing that the individual felt more relaxed and forgot about the criticism or told the criticizer off. Careful questioning by the group or by the leader prior to the group's starting might reveal difficulties in assertion and extreme sensitivity to criticism. Both of these problems would lend themselves to group treatment quite well and we shall provide some concrete examples of how in later sections.

The third and fourth drinking episodes in our example were drinking instead of eating dinner and drinking to get him going in the morning. Let us examine number three. If our patient or our home observer is keeping accurate records he would have recorded under the column, What Occurred Just Prior to Drinking?, "wife called out, 'Dinner is ready!' ". Then, he would have recorded the Date, Time, and specific room in his house for Place. Under the next column, Alone or Whom With?, he would have recorded, "with family". Next he would have recorded an estimate of the Amount Consumed and then the Type of Beverage. Finally, he would have recorded something under the last column, What Happened After Drinking?. He might have recorded something in this last column such as "I wasn't bothered by her voice anymore and I was glad she had cooked for me for nothing. Served her right". Again, looking at his intake pattern over time might demonstrate similar ways of escaping aversive stimulation, that his appetite diminishes when drinking, and that he uses alcohol to help him punish others, even when such punishment is not warranted (if his wife deserved punishment for anything, and that is debatable because of insufficient information, it would be for telling him to punish the kids when he arrived home and then punishing him when he failed to do so. Instead of counter-punishing her or asserting himself, however, he ended up punishing her surreptitiously for cooking dinner which was an appropriate behavior that he should have reinforced).

The fact that he had a drink or two the following morning "to get going" is not uncommon. The hangover sets the stage and functions as the cue. The drinking itself allows the patient to escape the aversive headache, nausea, criticism, etc. It is also not uncommon for alcoholics to continue drinking to avoid the onset of withdrawal symptoms entirely.

The last drinking episode mentioned, having several at lunch to "steady the nerves", was cued by making mistakes on the job, by people looking at him, and by worry over his job being in danger. Examining his intake pattern would probably show that each of these is sufficient to act as a cue for drinking. Group discussion could focus on steps he could take to increase his job security, and how he could be desensitized to making mistakes and having people look at him.

While we have been discussing an individual who claims that he does not know why he drinks, all of what we have demonstrated applies equally well to those who *can* tell us why they drink. Often large discrepancies exist between what the patient thinks alcohol is doing for him and his actual behavior just before and just after drinking. In addition, cues which set the stage for excessive drinking may be unnoticed, and it is easy to attribute the reasons to things which may have little to do with the total amount of drinking that goes on.

Reinforcement and Contracting

To reinforce is to present some verbal or physical reward after a response occurs. Anything is potentially a reinforcer. The only way one can be sure is to see the effect it has on the response which it follows: if it makes the response more likely to occur again under the same conditions, it is strengthening the behavior and is, therefore, a reinforcer. On the other hand, if a consequence to a response produces some verbal or physical event which decreases or suppresses the response, the event is punishing the behavior and is an aversive event. If drinking is followed by an Antabuse reaction, drinking is punished by that very aversive event.

It is easy to show that what may be reinforcing for one person in a group may be aversive to someone else. Someone who loves to talk and be the center of attention, for example, would probably talk at a very high rate (talking response strengthened) if the leader and the rest of the group sat and reinforced the talking behavior with rapt attention, continuous eye contact, nods of agreement, and requests for more detail. Another individual who finds talking in group aversive would probably talk as little as possible under the same conditions. Therefore, one should not assume that a reinforcer *is* a reinforcer until the effect has been observed.

Extinction refers to the process of withholding reinforcement from a response which has ordinarily been given reinforcement. The purpose of extinction is to diminish the response. If the group ignored an individual who had previously gained a great deal of attention by telling people how much liquor he can drink two things would happen. First, his rate of such talk would probably increase (this can be expected and is called the extinction burst) but, if the group remained steadfast, his alcohol talk would soon begin to decrease, especially if the group gave him attention when he spoke of other, more appropriate topics.

Reinforcement is most effective when it is delivered immediately. When a response is new and still weak and unpracticed, reinforce each time the response occurs. To make the response durable, however, the schedule of reinforcement should be *thinned* and reinforcement should be given every second or third time the response occurs. At the same time, patients need to learn how to start programming their own reinforcers for themselves as part of improving self-control.

A convenient vehicle for teaching patients to program their own reinforcers as well as for teaching realistic goal setting is a written contract. Homme *et al.* (1970), Knox (1971), and Stuart (1971) have described the procedure in detail on a one-to-one counseling basis. It is impossible, however, to make the same kinds of commitments to a group, or, to bring up a contract negotiated on a one-to-one basis in the group and to discuss the commitment.

Several steps are involved in teaching patients to write their own contracts. First, the therapist or group leader and the patient decide upon some specific problem behaviors which can be improved on a daily or weekly basis. A level of performance is then agreed upon which *both* parties agree is fair, easily attainable, clear, and worthwhile. Next, consequences in the form of reinforcement are agreed upon for performing the behavior at the specified level. Both parties must agree that the reinforcer(s) is acceptable in that it is given consistently and a short time after the performance. The contract should also be positive in the sense that the parties are saying, "If you do this I'll do that " vs. "I will not do this if you do that." The contract is considered fair if the amount of work required of both parties or the amount of performance and the amount of reinforcement are of equal weight.

The second and third stages of teaching patients to write their own contracts either with themselves or with family members involves showing them how to specify target behaviors clearly so that there is no doubt or room for argument as to whether they occurred or did not occur. The same is true for teaching the patient to identify reinforcers which are all around him but which are unnoticed and taken for granted. The patient is then given guided practice in writing contracts specifying first the behaviors and then the agreed upon consequences.

Exchange contracts between husband and wife are variations of self-contracting. They seek to teach partners how to reciprocally give in order to get and take the general form, "I'll do this if you'll do that". This is in contrast to a coercive or arbitrary form or interaction, for example, "Do it or else" or "Do it because I said so."

Contracts should be written, signed by both parties, and dated. The period for which the contract is in effect should be specified as well as when the contract will be reviewed for changes or extensions. In addition, there should be some provision for record keeping of the behaviors to occur. If the contract is negotiated between an individual and the group, all should sign and have access to copies. Progress toward performing the behaviors should be discussed in the group and support for following the contract given. Often it is helpful to provide fines or other consequences for failure to follow the contract in addition to the positive consequences for meeting the terms.

By writing and completing a series of short-term contracts, patients move toward specifying and attaining longer-term goals. Therefore, a fourth stage in contracting is teaching the patient to specify long-term goals and the methods by which he can attain them. While progress toward short-term goals is reinforced almost immediately with small rewards, this same progress and the same rewards are, in fact, serving the purpose of rewarding progress toward long-term goals. When a series of short-term or "mini" contracts is fulfilled, that in itself may be a long-term goal, and the reinforcer should be of greater magnitude than for each of the short-term contracts. To illustrate, a wife might want to redecorate or paint a house. The husband would like her to stop nagging him to do it. Both would like to take a vacation in a few months. A series of short-term exchange contracts might be as follows: Husband: I agree to paint for one hour during the week and at least four hours a day on weekends if my wife does not mention painting that day and if she gives me a choice of dinners for that evening. Wife: I agree to give my husband a choice of dinners and to not mention painting to him if he paints for one hour a day during the week and four hours a day on weekends. Additional consequences might also be specified in case of default: If my husband fails to paint the required number of hours on any day, he will prepare his own dinner and do his own dishes. The husband might add: If my wife mentions painting or does not provide a choice of dinners I will not be required to paint that day. Both the husband and the wife may then agree to a longer term goal: If the house is completed by (date) we will take a week's vacation in Canada.

Shaping, Fading and Prompting Responses

Shaping refers to a procedure in which a new response is learned by rewarding rough approximations to the desired response. An individual who has never been in a group before and who is unable to discuss intimate material can be reinforced initially just for talking. As time goes on, however, he can be prompted by the leader (who also prompts the rest of the group to do the same) for talk which comes closer and closer to the desired areas for discussion. As the desired responses are made and strengthened through group support and reinforcement, the leader fades his prompts out of the picture and lets the natural contingencies of reinforcement take over.

Psychodrama Techniques

A variety of techniques using principles of social learning theory have evolved. Many have been with us for years under different names. Moreno (1966), for example, has developed several techniques within the general context of psychodrama. Sturm (1970, 1965) has translated these techniques into a behavioral format. While space does not permit a full discussion of all Moreno's techniques, some of the more frequently used techniques as they relate to a behaviorally oriented group will be presented.

Warm-up is a period in which the leader attempts to elicit a great deal of reinforcing interaction (smiles, acceptance, physical touching, attentive listening) and to discourage punishment or extinction (bored stares, disapproval, withdrawal). An atmosphere is created in which participation in the group and the group itself is seen as reinforcing, and people can be spontaneous without fear of punishment.

Problem-presentation begins with the leader reinforcing the members' attempts to reveal personal problems which they are asking the group to help solve. Usually a problem is focused on what the group agrees is relevant to their own lives. Often the leader serves as a model for members to imitate by stating that everyone, even he, has problems with which to contend.

Self-presentation is the next step in which the individual describes the setting and characters in detail in which the problem has most recently come up. The leader may also ask the individual to enact the various roles so that all present can get a better understanding of the cues which set the stage for various responses and what the consequences are.

Role-playing techniques are probably the most widely used of all those to come from psychodrama. They enable group members to model appropriate behavior for others to imitate, to selectively prompt and reinforce each other for improved performance, and to see oneself from others' points of view.

After self-presentation of the problem, the leader asks the patient to choose members from the group to play the major characters. In choosing the auxiliary cast, the patient is asked to choose whenever possible on the basis of an actual resemblance to a real character. In addition, the auxiliaries are told to incorporate their own reactions into the role. If they are not quite sure of how to play them, additional detail is given and several trial runs are made. Often the patient is asked to reverse roles either to show how the character needs to be played or to show the patient the other's position or point of view. When roles are reversed again to their original positions, patients often have new ideas of how best to respond to the other individual, taking into account the other's expectations and perceptions.

Not only does role-reversal enable patients to understand better the behavior of others, but it also provides an opportunity for the patient to interact with "himself." By stepping back and looking at himself, patients are often surprised at their own behavior and are often quite receptive to prompts and suggestions from other group members as to how to handle the problem differently. These alternate ways of handling situations can then be rehearsed and re-rehearsed with the group providing feedback as to how comfortable, convincing, and appropriate the patient seems in performing the new behaviors.

Sometimes it is apparent that the patient is responding to cues or consequences which other members of the group feel are not there. Or, it may be that the group senses that the patient is avoiding saying or doing certain things which would be most appropriate. A technique for giving this feedback immediately and, at the same time modeling the appropriate behavior, is *doubling*. The leader asks one or more group members to play directly along-side the patient and to first mimic his responses in order to start approximating his character. The next step is the dropping of simple mimicry when the auxiliary is ready and saying and doing what the patient is not saying and doing under the circumstances. The patient stops his enactment to observe the double and then imitates the double's behavior. He then observes the consequences of the new behavior on the character with which he is interacting. He can also reverse roles at this point to compare his old behavior with the new behavior learned from the double.

While the double provides instant and simultaneous feedback of new behavior to be learned and imitated, the *mirror* is the original "instant replay" developed long before video tape equipment. The patient is asked to leave the stage or area where role-playing is occurring and to watch while an auxiliary plays parts of the performance just enacted. The patient can then evaluate his performance while not in the midst of some other role. The auxiliary may also be requested by the leader to extend the new behaviors to new situations so that the patient can see the adequacy of his new responses in a variety of settings. In *Future Projection* the patient and other group members anticipate problems and practice solutions using the new behaviors for future events which are likely to occur or which the patient would like to see occur.

Sessions are usually brought to an end with additional reinforcement for the patient who enacted his problems and for the group as a whole. This is accomplished through *Group Participation* in which group members are called upon to share what they learned about their own problems while observing the enactments and providing feedback. In this way tangible progress is made public, and the patient is reinforced for his efforts by knowing that he helped others in the group.

Assertion Training.

This technique, developed by Wolpe (1958), involves training patients to appropriately express both positive and negative feelings. It is common for many of us to say nothing rather than to stick up for our rights or to tell someone off because of fear. Either we are afraid of hurting their feelings or we are uncomfortable because we do not know quite how to say it. Often feelings of resentment keep building and the fear of losing control and "blowing up" develops. In these cases, alcohol enables the individual to either relax and forget the resentment or to tell the person what he thinks of them (with guilt and apologies often following when sober).

Assertion problems are frequently apparent when group members seem timid, relate experiences in which they did not know what to say, and have trouble expressing positive feelings such as love and respect as well as annoyance, irritation, and expressions of the opinion that their rights as human beings have been infringed upon. Role-playing techniques can be extremely useful in assessing the problem and treating it.

The leader, for example, can openly ask the group if any members have difficulty telling people how they feel or if they "keep things inside." If no one volunteers such information, standard scenes can be enacted with group members taking turns in the various roles and giving each other feedback as to how they come across. Wolpe asks patients to respond to such standard scenes as: walking out of a shop and finding you have been short-changed one dollar; someone pushing in front of you in line; ordering a steak rare and the waiter brings it well done. Wolpe and Lazarus (1966, p. 41) provide a more complete list of possibilities. Additional scenes can be used, depending on the actual experiences of group members once it has been established that some members really do have an assertion problem.

Desensitization

Systematic desensitization is another technique developed by Wolpe for the treatment of a specific problem, namely, excessive fear which prevents appropriate behavior from occurring. While the technique was originally employed in individual therapy as was assertion training, it has been successfully used in groups on many occasions. We must, however, make a distinction between groups formed purely for desensitization, assertion, or some other specific problem and more heterogeneous groups which include these techniques for some members. It is probably unwise to spend very much group time on a problem which has relevance only for a very few members, and, therefore, unless the problem involves a theme which is troublesome for other members, too, and can be treated in a few sessions of role-playing, it is better to form another group for individuals just having that problem. An alternative would be to deal with it in individual therapy.

As originally developed, systematic desensitization involved first, pinpointing precisely what it is about the situation which is causing the fear, and what factors seem to make it better or worse. For example, a patient might become panicky if criticized by his boss in front of co-workers but only a little uncomfortable if criticized about his bowling score by friends. A hierarchy of scenes is drawn up ranging from the first scene which causes no discomfort at all to the last scene which makes the patient the most frightened which that problem has made him. To insure that steps between hierarchy items are not too great, the patient is asked to rate each scene on a subjective 100 point scale. The zero point represents absolute calm and one hundred represents the most frightened he has been. Hierarchy items, according to Wolpe, should not be any more than 15 units apart.

Patients are then taught *deep muscle relaxation* which is believed to be a response incompatible with fear and which is a very useful technique in its own right for individuals who have trouble relaxing. After relaxation is achieved, the patient imagines himself actually engaged in the first scene on the hierarchy. The scene is imagined several times first three to five seconds, then six to eight seconds and then usually ten to twelve seconds. Relaxation is reinstated between each imagining. If no anxiety is signaled while imagining, the process is repeated with the next scene until the entire hierarchy is negotiated, a process which usually takes several months.

Often relaxation training and a small amount of *in vivo* desensitization can be easily incorporated into a group which has not been formed specifically for those reasons. Desensitization often is a by-product of role-playing almost any new behavior until it feels comfortable and can be accomplished by shaping and rewarding approximations to the goal behavior. For example, an individual with a fear of criticism can construct a hierarchy with the help of the group and then role-play each scene until it no longer causes discomfort. Each step in the hierarchy represents approximations to the final scene which may be a goal to then achieve outside the group. The group may actually give individual members homework assignments to carry out between meetings. One of these can be reporting on doing those things outside the group which the member has been working on in the group. It is important, however, not to give assignments which the member is not ready for or which will lead to failure. Members should not go beyond the hierarchy scene they have successfully completed in group.

Another way of doing systematic desensitization, assertion training, and relaxation training in groups is to carefully select group members who have one of those problems and work only on that problem in that group. Lazarus (1961, 1968), for example, describes group desensitization and assertion training. More recently Suinn and Richardson (1971) have developed an extension of relaxation training to provide a general competency for new anxiety provoking situations. These groups are time-limited and highly specific. The members all have the same problem, although they may be heterogeneous in other respects such as age, educational background, etc. For example, in a desensitization group, all the members might have a fear of height for which they are seeking treatment. In a ward of alcoholic patients there may be a half-dozen or more who have fears of failure or other specific fears. Often highly specific groups can be run simultaneously with other groups and individual therapy in a general ongoing alcohol treatment program. Frequent staff meetings are necessary to insure continuity of care across modalities.

Relaxation Training

First introduced by Jacobson in 1938, the procedure is relatively straightforward and can be mastered by most people in a few hours of training. There is considerable overlap with hypnotic techniques, especially some of the suggestions which some clinicians use to deepen the state of relaxation achieved. Each of the major muscle groups in the body is first tensed and then slowly relaxed beginning with the hands and forearm. The fist is clenched and the patient is asked to concentrate on the feeling of tension and to learn to discriminate when it is present in varying degrees in each muscle group. Similarly, he is asked to concentrate on the feeling of relaxation which seems to "flow into the muscle" when, after being held tense for about 5 seconds, it is slowly relaxed. The upper arms are usually done after the hands and forearms: the triceps by pushing the hands against each other very hard and gradually relaxing and the biceps by clenching the fist and tensing the upper arm and gradually relaxing. The muscles of the upper back, neck, face, stomach, thighs, calves, and ankles are all done in like fashion. If any tension remains in any muscle, the patient is instructed to redo it until it feels quite relaxed. A calm, relaxing voice on the part of the therapist is required, as is a quiet room with no distractions. While a reclining chair or couch is optimal, I have relaxed groups of eight patients on hard folding chairs by having them get as comfortable as possible by leaning way back with legs outstretched, head back, and eyes closed. No muscle tension should be required to sit or recline while listening to the instructions and arms should be resting comfortably at the sides.

After the muscles have been relaxed, additional suggestions are given. For example, patients can be told to concentrate on their breathing: "Breathe deeply . . . (pause while patients inhale) and slowly . . . calm and relaxed. Muscles loose . . . no hurry . . . enjoying the relaxation you have achieved. Notice how you seem to get heavier in the chair and muscles seem to relax more each time you exhale." Another common suggestion is to ask patients to imagine lying in the sun and to feel the warmth of the sun on their skin. "Your muscles feel warm and relaxed. You may find yourself getting a little drowsy. Perhaps you can hear water lapping against the side of a pool." Another useful technique is to ask patients to think of a word which they can associate with the pleasant state of relaxation (not an alcohol related word) and which they can think of when they are beginning to feel tense. Patients are told to practice relaxation between sessions in order to achieve it more rapidly. When proficiency is gained the patient merely thinks of his word or tells himself to relax.

In concluding this section on techniques and terminology, several words of caution are needed. It should be obvious to the reader that we have merely scratched the surface of techniques and procedures about which many volumes have been written and into which many years of research and development have gone. Readers should have some knowledge of the existence of these techniques from the foregoing section, but they are urged to consult both the references listed and other practitioners who have some experience using the techniques. No technique is effective if used incorrectly.

PRE-GROUP PREPARATIONS

Selection

There are many opinions as to whom to select for a group and whom to exclude. Almost all writers agree that at the very least, members should be able to listen to each other and be able to talk to each other. Aside from this basic and obvious starting point, group leaders differ markedly. Some prefer only highly motivated and highly verbal members having a great deal of similarity in problem areas. Others prefer the most heterogeneous group possible. In dealing with alcoholism, the author's preference is for a heterogeneous group in regard to age, sex, educational level, length of alcoholism and related problems, marital status and verbal ability. On the other hand, extremes in socio-economic and educational areas are probably best avoided.

Usually the author will form a homogeneous group when, as mentioned earlier, several individuals are found to share a very specific problem such as assertion or relaxation. The homogeneity centers around the problem area itself rather than around personality characteristics of the members.

When in doubt about the composition of a group and the selection of members, it may be useful to run a larger trial group first (Stone, Parloff, and Frank, 1954). Members for smaller groups can then be drawn, based on the performance of individuals in the trial group and the leader's criteria for membership.

Size

The author has found that a group of from six to eight members is optimal. Other writers would tend to agree (e.g., Goldstein, Heller, and Sechrest, 1966).

Assessment

Closely related to the selection problem is the problem of assessing individual difficulties which might be effectively dealt with in a group setting. We have already discussed several important aspects of assessment, a functional analysis of behavior and objective data on the frequency, duration, or magnitude of appropriate and inappropriate responses. The goal is to identify behavioral assets as well as deficits and excesses and to get some indication of functioning in these areas prior to treatment.

Several other instruments and procedures are used in addition to the Intake Record. First, there is probably no substitute for a thorough interview. The author uses an intake interview which asks for four collateral sources of information for reliability and validity checks, demographic information in terms of number of days worked, highest monthly income, number of days spent in jail or in a hospital for alcohol related problems, how serious a problem alcohol is, and family history and living conditions, for the six months prior to entering treatment. This information is later compared to what is occurring six months after treatment. The information also tells a great deal about the individual factually and in the way he answers the questions.

Frequently the Fear Survey Schedule (Wolpe and Lang, 1964; see Tasto *et al.*, 1970 for an updated version with norms) is administered. The Schedule is a checklist of 122 items which sometimes arouse fear or discomfort. Patients are asked to indicate how much discomfort they would feel to each item on a five point scale ranging from "Not at All" to "Very Much." Often the Schedule provides information regarding fear arousing cues or situations which lead to heavy drinking. Areas covered include social situations, medical procedures, and small animals and insects.

Another paper and pencil technique which is sometimes used is the Reinforcer Survey Schedule (Cautela and Kastenbaum, 1967). The Schedule, which by no means exhausts all possibilities, attempts to identify activities (other than drinking) which patients might enjoy. Group dscussion can often focus on these other possibilities.

On occasion, particularly when there is question of thought disorder, some traditional diagnostic tests such as the MMPI, Memory-for-Designs, and Proverbs might be used. However, if thought disorder fails to appear in the hour long intake interview, it is doubtful that there is enough present to preclude an individual from participating in a group. Kanfer and Saslow (1969) provide a more detailed discussion of behavioral assessment techniques used in conjunction with more traditional methods.

Time Limits

Depending on the context in which the group occurs, there are probably advantages in both time-limited and time-unlimited groups. Time-limited groups are often useful when maximum gains are sought in least amount of time, when progress and goals are explicit, waiting lists long, when treatment needs to be standardized (as for example, in process and outcome research), and problems are not so severe as to be expected to take more than two to six months to resolve. Time limits may also bring pressure to bear on individuals "to start shaping up" as the end of therapy approaches and slower members see tangible gains made by other members in the group.

An alternative approach which combines an ongoing group format with time-limited therapy is one in which individuals enter and leave the ongoing group when they have reached their criterion levels of performance or the goals they set for themselves with the help of the leader and the rest of the group. Thus, in the pre-group assessment and specification of problems, a timetable of expected progress and termination can also be tentatively formulated. This does not mean that goals and timetables cannot be revised as new problem behaviors become apparent in the group. Nor does it mean that other group members cannot assist in revising goals, problem solving strategies, and timetables once the group has begun. On the contrary, both are desirable and should be prompted and reinforced.

GROUP MEETINGS

Initial sessions are usually spent establishing ground rules or reiterating those discussed in pre-group meetings with the leader, refining assessment techniques and problems to be worked on, and restating the implied or written treatment contract.

Common ground rules include such matters as promptness, the expectation that members will try to help each other, that what goes on in the group is confidential*, that relationships among members outside the group should be discussed in the group, that assignments outside the group will be completed and reported on in the group, and that private meetings with the leader can be requested at any time but that what is discussed should be brought up in group either by the patient when he feels he is ready, or by the leader when he feels the patient is ready. Another ground rule is often that members cannot attend group if they have been drinking, but that urges to drink are appropriate to discuss in the group**. This is more frequently a needed rule with outpatients rather than inpatients.

Additions, deletions, and modifications to these rules are often the topic of the first meetings. They can be used as vehicles to get members "warmed up" to talking in the group. By reinforcing and prompting this somewhat impersonal, but interesting and constructive material, the leader begins making the group itself more attractive. As the attractiveness of the group increases, so does its potential for helping through reinforcement of appropriate within-and extra-group activity. During these initial meetings, the leader also prompts and models much verbal behavior which emphasizes the commonalities among the members and avoids or discourages interactions which might be aversive (see earlier section on warm-up).

Unless members begin discussing problems spontaneously, the leader begins prompting the group to start doing this. He may ask someone to begin who seemed quite willing to share his problems with the group in pre-group meetings. The individual may be asked to recount

---

*Confidentiality can be a problem in regard to other staff within an institution who are responsible for the patient but who may not be members of a particular group. Sometimes patients will not discuss material which they are afraid will be entered in charts for others who are less familiar to them to read. Often these fears can be allayed by assuring patients that other staff are professionals who are there to help, or that the information will be charted in very general terms or not at all until the patient feels he is ready to share it with those staff.

**While problems which result in urges to drink are discussed, "drink talk" *per se* is discouraged at least in later sessions. Examples of "drink talk" would be humorous descriptions of events which happened while drunk, favorite beverages, or boasts of how much liquor one can hold. This type of material contributes nothing constructive except, perhaps, to remind us that the individual needs to develop social skills in other areas.

some of the problems he and the leader discussed, perhaps Intake Record data or perhaps a contract he is thinking of negotiating with his wife. This, in turn, leads to discussions of whether or not others in the group have similar problems, how they are typically handled, how they can be handled differently, and how group members can help. The leader, meanwhile, should be prompting and modeling problem solving strategies and reinforcing the group for generating solutions to problems. Potential solutions are role-played with the group providing feedback as to how adequate and comfortable the characters appear. As the leader prompts and reinforces the group for appropriate behavior, the group imitates him, especially if this process is made explicit and the group is encouraged to do so. As the group imitates the leader's behavior, the leader can begin fading his prompts and reinforcements and allow the group more and more autonomy. Sessions can be closed with a review of progress and assignments to try some of the rehearsed behavior outside the group and to record the results.

Later meetings can begin with a summary by a member of what happened at the last meeting. This in itself may create fruitful discussion since other members may have different perceptions and remembrances of what occurred. Next, a presentation of what occurred outside the group since the last meeting usually ensues with questions directed at those who had assignments to carry out in the interim. Throughout, the leader must keep the group on its course, the generation and maintenance of new behavior.

It is not uncommon for individuals to begin manifesting behavior within the group which serves the purpose of allowing the individuals to avoid certain subject areas. Fidgeting, extreme nervousness, pacing, lateness, very much or very little talking, monopolizing the group, competing for the leader's attention, long discussions of personal history, complaints of mistreatment are some of the typical group behaviors which may cause the group to drift off course. Usually bringing these episodes to the group's attention brings censure to the individuals responsible. The inappropriate behaviors may then decrease or they may be denied. In either case, the wishes of the group can be made explicit and the guilty parties can then be asked by the group for a commitment to decrease those distracting behaviors while increasing other appropriate behaviors. These within-group behaviors also provide additional information for problem areas to be worked on. Cases of extreme nervousness or too little talking, for example, might indicate the need for relaxation training or assertion training.

As the group progresses, new goals might be substituted for those originally discussed. As the new behaviors are learned and practiced outside the group, it becomes obvious that the group becomes less and less necessary for certain individuals. The fact that someone is getting ready to terminate should be explicit. This gives the group a chance to provide feedback to the individual as to the progress they have seen him make and to reinforce the individual's self-confidence. The individual, in turn, can give the group feedback on how they have helped him. Rather than terminating abruptly, it is probably better for most individuals to gradually phase out by attending less and less frequently, using the group to support and reinforce the new behaviors being carried out outside the group and by functioning as a model for other patients to imitate.

CONCLUSION

Many techniques have been presented within a behavioral context. These techniques can be used regardless of the reader's theoretical orientation simply by translating the terminology into language with which the reader is most familiar and using those techniques that seem to make the most sense in a given situation. It would probably be most effective for the novice group leader to choose a few techniques at first and become thoroughly proficient with them before trying to master a large number. Otherwise, the resulting groups will be a hodgepodge of technique while common sense and just plain listening will be minimal.

REFERENCES

Cautela, J. R., and Kastenbaum, R. A.: A reinforcement survey schedule for use in therapy, training and research. *Psychological Reports, 20:*1115-1130, 1967.

Goldstein, A. P., Heller, K., and Sechrest, L. B.: *Psychotherapy and the Psychology of Behavior Change.* New York, Wiley, 1966.

Jackson, D., and Della-Piana, G.: Establishing a behavioral observation system: A self-instruction program. Unpublished manuscript, Bureau of Educational Research, University of Utah, 1971.

Homme, L., Csanyi, A. P., Gonzales, Mary Ann, and Rechs, J. R.: *How to*

Use Contingency Contracting in the Classroom. Champaign, Research Press, 1970.

Kanfer, F. H., and Saslow, G:. Behavioral diagnosis. In Franks, C.M. (Ed.): *Behavior Therapy: Appraisal and status,* New York, McGraw-Hill, 1969, pp. 417-444.

Knox, D.: *Marriage Happiness: A Behavioral Approach to Counseling.* Champaign, Research Press, 1971.

Lazarus, A. A.: Group therapy of phobic disorders by systematic desensitization. *Journal of Abnormal and Social Psychology, 63:*504-510, 1961.

Lazarus, A. A.: Behavior therapy in groups. In Gazda, G. M. (Ed.): *Basic Approaches to Group Psychotherapy and Counseling.* Springfield, Thomas, 1968, pp. 149-175.

Moreno, Z. T.: Psychodramatic rules, techniques, and adjunctive methods. *Psycho-drama and psychotherapy.* New York, Beacon, 1966.

Stone, A. R., Parloff, M. B., and Frank, J. D.: The use of "diagnostic groups" in a group therapy program. *International Journal of Gorup Psychotherapy, 4:*274, 1954.

Stuart, R. B.: Behavioral contracting within the families of delinquents. *Journal of Behavior Therapy and Experimental Psychiatry, 2:*1-11, 1971.

Sturm, I. E.: The behavioristic aspect of psychodrama. *Group Psychotherapy, 18:*50-64, 1965.

Sturm, I. E.: A behavioral outline of psychodrama. *Psychotherapy: Theory, Research and Practice, 7:*245-247, 1970.

Suinn, R. M., and Richardson, F.: Anxiety management training: A nonspecific behavior therapy program for anxiety control. *Behavior Therapy, 2:*498-510, 1971.

Tasto, D. L., and Hickson, R.: Standardization and scaling of the 122-item fear survey schedule. *Behavior Therapy, 1:*473-484, 1970.

Wolpe, J.: *Psychotherapy by Reciprocal Inhibition.* Stanford, Stanford University Press, 1958.

Wolpe, J., and Lang, P. J.: A fear survey schedule for use in behavior therapy *Behavior Research and Therapy, 2:*27-30, 1964.

Wolpe, J., and Lazarus, A. A.: *Behavior Therapy Techniques.* New York, Pergamon, 1966.

CHAPTER VIII

GROUP WORK THROUGH PEER PRESSURE: A THERAPEUTIC APPROACH TO THE REHABILITATION OF THE YOUTHFUL DRUG ABUSER

JOHN G. CULL AND RICHARD E. HARDY

APPROXIMATELY THREE years ago, the SEED was founded in Fort Lauderdale, Florida, by Art and Shelly Barker. The basic design of the program is the general treatment model developed by Alcoholics Anonymous; however, there are several modalities which are peculiar to the SEED. The description which follows is basically an outline of the goals and methods of the program; however, certain intangibles which are difficult to describe exist in the program.

The SEED was developed because of a desperate need for help which existed for young people in the Fort Lauderdale area as a result of the heightened incidence of drug abuse. It was felt that new approaches to the problem were needed; therefore, the SEED concept evolved. The SEED program's concept was based on the premise that man can change his behavior and can live and cope in his environment. The young people who seek help from the SEED program learn that they can no longer "cop out" with drugs; but that they have daily problems and must learn to live with them. At the SEED, they obtain a sense of belonging to something meaningful along with the knowledge that they can find purpose in their lives with the extra ingredient—a sense of dedication toward helping themselves and helping others to help themselves. The primary function of the SEED program is to provide rehabilitative services for the young person who has become a drug experimenter, user, abuser, or addict.

APPLICATION CRITERIA

The SEED is made available to anyone needing help. The addict who must have some sort of maintenance—such as Methadone—to assist him in achieving detoxification will not be accepted by the SEED until such time as he is able to tolerate a truly "cold turkey" program of abstinence. Since its main program is not detoxification, the aim is to work with the experimenter, user, abuser, or addict who has used drugs less than ten years. Because of the age range— nine years to early twenties—parental consent of the majority of applicants is needed.

Anyone seeking help from the SEED and in need of detoxification treatment is referred to the appropriate facilities. Those applicants who are in need of medical attention are referred to appropriate hospitals and/or their private physicians. These young people then come back to the SEED program once they are considered to be in sound medical health. Other than these selected criteria, the SEED makes no distinction concerning participation in the program.

Physical discomfort of "withdrawal" is at a minimum among participants. Even those young people who have used heroin for two or more years and have $200-a-day habits (this is equivalent to $60 to $65 in New York) take only approximately three days to pass through withdrawal symptoms.

BACKGROUND OF THE PROGRAM PARTICIPANTS

A unique factor of the SEED program is that it reaches into the schools. In this community, estimates show that between 70 and 85 percent of the children are experimenting with, using, or abusing drugs. The SEED has been successful in reaching young people throuugh referrals made by principals, teachers, and counselors of the various schools in Broward County. The apparent change in students using drugs such as the decline of grades, failures, and dropouts, along with attitude change has added to the frustration and dilemma of educators. Due to the referrals made by educators to the SEED program, the majority of the young people destined to become delinquents and burdens on society have been able to continue in school education and to aid teachers in understanding the drug problems of the young. The young abuser is of considerable help in helping other drug abusers since he understands not only the values but also the language of the drug culture (Hardy and Cull, 1973).

Many young people, no matter how well they progress, have environmental backgrounds which make their personal adjustment almost impossible. If there is no reinforcement from the family, the young person will meet constantly with disappointment and discouragement. For those young people in this particular situation, the SEED has been able to assist with the cooperation of either the courts and/or various agencies (vocational rehabilitation, family services, etc.) in obtaining foster homes and has been successful in continuing to work with them in their new environments.

SERVICE DELIVERY SYSTEM

The first phase of the SEED's program consists, in most cases, of a two-week program of intensive group discussions, but this phase is expandable when the need exists. During this two-week period, the group discussion sessions average approximately twelve hours per day. In these sessions, the participant is aided in gaining insight into what he is and what he has done to his life by taking drugs; but more importantly, he learns what his life can be for him and the impact he can have on others if he is *straight*. These two weeks represent the equivalent in time of the participant's going to a psychologist and/or psychiatrist for a period of three years on a one-hour, once-a-week basis. The 14-day intensive group sessions provide a radical and comprehensive change which facilitates the learning process of the participant. The SEED is operated on a continuous seven-day week basis. The participant in this 14-day program is at the SEED from 10 A.M. to 10 P.M., during which time he is involved constantly in "rap" sessions under the supervision of staff. These rap sessions are carefully guided and the intensity is maintained at a controlled, effective level. When necessary for certain individual needs, "rap" sessions also are held on a one-to-one basis with a staff member.

Upon successful completion of this first phase, an additional three-month period ensues which requires the participant to attend four group sessions a week. This phase of the program offers practical application of his learning processes. He learns to function and cope in his environment while returning to the group involvement. The criteria of success of this program are based not only on the fact that the young person is drug free, but also on his attitude change toward life; that is, there is a love of self and others, community and country, and a sense of dedication to help his fellow man.

Due to the age of participants, they can adjust well to change. The amount of attitude change in the individual seems to indicate that the three-month period is quite effective. In some instances, individuals require either an extension of the two-week period or an extension of the three-months' program. Periodic follow-up is done to see how the participants are doing.

If the participant learns well and grasps the meaning of honesty, love, respect, discipline, and affection, there is no need for him to go back to drugs. For the young people who are found to have deep-rooted psychological or serious physical problems, the SEED makes referrals to medical doctors, psychologists, and/or other community programs. This is true particularly during the individual's participation in the two-week intensive program.

Up until his introduction to the SEED, the *druggie's* best, most reliable friend has been the lie that he speaks and lives in order to mislead his parents and his teachers. This same lie directed to a staff member at the SEED is guaranteed to trigger a *choicely worded* verbal barrage not soon to be forgotten. The reason for this is that the staff member is a former *druggie* himself and can easily detect a falsehood.

Because it is tough to lose an old friend—and the lie has been his best friend—it must be replaced with something of at least equal value. This is where the SEED asserts its true strength and individuality Just after the above-described verbal barrage, the staff member will close the one-on-one session by saying to the thoroughly deflated individual, "I love you". No one who has heard this shopworn phrase as it is spoken at the SEED can fail to be deeply moved by the sincerity and purpose behind its use. The reinforcing effect of true concern (love) is quite awesome.

The success of the SEED program also depends largely on family participation. The families are encouraged to attend two meetings a week to participate with the young people. Through this participation, the parents can get an overall picture of what the SEED is about and can see the gradual improvement of not only their own children but also those of other parents. They also can acquaint themselves with these other parents.

The group participation of parents and children, particularly those parents who are deeply involved with the program, has produced remarkable results in that the family unit is brought closer together and gains a better understanding of the dynamics of its problem. Also it has been observed that a greater level of compassion evolves within the family.

Fundamental to the continuing success of the SEED's program—especially during the period immediately following the two-week initial phase—is a highly effective intelligence network put together by Art Barker, which is composed of ex-druggies, teachers, police, and concerned friends. If an apparently rehabilitated participant is seen even talking with an unreconstructed acquaintance, Mr. Barker knows about it in a matter of minutes and is able to get help to the offender.

STAFFING AND TRAINING

The SEED has been able to train group leaders and help them develop talents of leadership. It also has been successful in encouraging these group leaders to continue more intensively in all endeavors to help combat the drug problem in the Fort Lauderdale area.

The SEED is strictly a paraprofessional organization with its group leaders and staff coming from the program. Because of its uniqueness, the quality of staffing can be maintained only on this basis. Art Barker is responsible for the overall operation of the program and for seeing that the outline and guidelines which have been developed are followed and the objectives fulfilled. He also is responsible for seeing that the other personnel maintain a high level of proficiency in meeting their obligations and fulfilling job requirements. Additionally, he is a liaison officer with other agencies in the community to effect cooperation and corrdinate efforts that benefit the community maximally without duplicating existing services.

There are four senior group leaders whose responsibility is to maintain group supervision when groups are in session. They assist in training new group leaders and junior group leaders. The junior group leaders are individuals who have gained some insight into the workings of the SEED program, but as yet have not developed the maturity or had experience which would prepare them to take a major responsibility for the conduct of either the initial intensive group sessions or the latter therapeutic group sessions. As they gain responsibility, they move on to being senior group leaders and assume a role of deeper responsibility. The staff of the SEED program, 25 paid and 15 volunteers, can effectively handle the approximately three hundred active participants in the program.

IMPACT AND RESULTS

The SEED has had a demonstrable impact in the Fort Lauderdale area. Its program has reached into the courts, the jails, the minority ghetto areas, and the schools of Broward County. The Broward County Personnel Association officially has adopted the SEED as its 1971 drug project and is assisting in obtaining employment for the successful young people while in, as well as when leaving, the SEED program. The district supervisor of the Florida Parole and Probation Office and his staff have been playing a vital role in the rehabilitation of these people during and after their participation in the SEED program. The SEED also uses resources such as Broward General Hospital, Henderson Clinic, Family Services, community services vocational rehabilitation, and adult education on an emergency and a referral basis. The SEED recently became a member of the Cooperative Areas Manpower Planning System (CAMPS) which is sponsored by the local city governments of Fort Lauderdale and Broward County. CAMPS is attempting to create a force of local agencies to effectively coordinate and cooperate in employment-developing opportunities. One role of the SEED is that of rehabilitating young people, enabling them to become employable and constructive members of society and their community; therefore, involvement with these other social agencies is essential.

It is interesting that the professionals who visit the SEED to observe the program seem to elevate different factors to prominence. One man might be struck by the obvious affection which permeates relationships between staff and participants; another by the sense of discipline displayed, and a third by the basic honesty of the program.

We feel the most effective factor influencing the youthful drug abuser at the SEED is peer pressure. The youthful ex-drugee is a potent influence in exerting conformity behavior. Cull (1971) has shown the peer pressure is influencial even among schizophrenics who have rejected interaction with the social world in a manner somewhat similar to the members of the drug culuture. Social roles are changing rapidly. No longer do the elders in our culture exert the impact on behavior and judgments they did in the past (Cull, 1970); consequently, the SEED has turned to the group which can exert sufficient social pressure to change behavior—youthful ex-drugees.

The drug dependence problem is one of the most pressing in the country, and Broward County is no exception. This is evidenced primarily by arrests, particularly of the youth between ages 13 and 20. The SEED's records substantiate this age span and document the fact that many youths start on drugs at an early age and advance from marijuana to hard narcotics within one year. In an effort to combat the drug problem, the SEED was founded approximately two years ago. The basic model for the program is the general treatment program developed by Alcoholics Anonymous, with some very important modifications.

The counselors or staff members are rehabilitated drug offenders. After having gone through the program themselves, they have been judged to have the necessary skills and motivations to assist in helping others. These skills consist basically of the ability to develop an empathic relationship with others and themselves, and finally, the ability to become skillful and successful group leaders. The group sessions may be categorized loosely with the more formal Guided Group Interaction and Transactional Analysis type groups. In the sessions of the SEED, both formal and informal group pressures are brought to bear upon the individual members by other members and leaders. As may be expected, it takes a very skillful leader to know when and how to apply pressure to any particular member of any particular segment of the group. This leader also must know how to channel the group's pressure to effective and fruitful endeavors. The group leaders are adept at reading the character of each member and then applying or halting the pressures. Having once been drug offenders themselves, they are able to pierce the protective shell which each drug offender throws over himself. The group leaders refuse to fall into the verbal and the cognitive traps which the drug offender sets. In the language of Transactional Analysis, the leaders see the games drug abusers may be playing and refuse to play them. They then point out to the individual how false ideas have led him to his present state of affairs.

The atmosphere where this guided group interaction takes place contains simply *affection, empathy, discipline,* and *love.* This *love* is a powerful tool in the hands of skilled leaders. In social power terms, the leader has been endowed referent power by the other members of the group. While at no time will he deny any group member, he does, however, skillfully manage the application of power. He uses his power to maintain motivation by reassuring those members who may have just received the brunt of a group session.

The above-described atmosphere of love has been coupled with the skillful handling of guided group interactions to form the SEED's unique and highly successful program. A new member attends two full weeks of twelve-hour sessions. If he has not made adequate progress, he may continue for two more weeks. Once a member has shown that he is responding, he is then allowed to return home. Prior to this he has stayed in the home of another participant and has gone to school or work from that home. After finishing this period, he returns to SEED for further group sessions every night for three hours and all day Saturday. This process lasts for three months. The member is then *straight* and attends only once or twice a week from then on.

During the day, there are two separate groups—one for males, the other for females. Particular problems are discussed and solutions found. In the evening, there is a general session which every member attends. The staff members take turns leading the discussion and help each other whenever necessary. Twice a week there is an open session in which parents, friends, teachers, probation and parole officers, and concerned others participate. At the open meetings, there are usually about 250 members and up to 400 visitors.

An essential element in the success of the SEED is the amount of community participation and aid. Referrals to the SEED program come through many channels. Some are self-referrals, others come because of parental or peer pressure. The various courts are probating individuals to the SEED and sometimes send an individual to it for a pre-sentence diagnostic type study. Many individuals, of course, come because of the attention of concerned adults such as relatives, teachers, and police officials. The SEED, because of its unique method and unequaled success ratio (now claimed to be over 90 percent), has managed to gather full community support.

SUMMARY

In summary, the SEED is an organization of former drug offenders who are dedicated to helping others. Its program of guided group interaction, honesty, concern, and understanding seems to have meshed into a workable method. The testimony of parents, doctors, friends, teachers, prison officials, members of school boards, and others all point to the fact that the SEED is a viable, dynamic program.

REFERENCES

Berne, Eric: *Transactional Analysis in Psychotherpy*. New York, Grove Press, 1961.

Cull, J. G.: Age as a factor in achieving conformity behavior. *Journal of Industrial Gerontology,* Spring, 1970.

Cull, J. G.: Conformity behavior in schizophrenics. *Journal of Social Psychology, 117:,* July 1971.

Hardy, R. E. and Cull, J. G.: Language of the drug abuser. In Hardy, R.E., and Cull, J. G. (Eds.): *Drug Dependence and Rehabilitation Approaches.* Springfield, Thomas, 1973.

Urbanik, Richard: Report on the SEED: a working drug treatment program in Fort Lauderdale, Florida. Department of Correction, State of North Carolina, 1971 (unpublished).

CHAPTER IX

THE USE OF GROUP COUNSELING IN ACHIEVING ADJUSTMENT TO WORK

ROBERT A. LASSITER

Purpose of This Chapter   Group Counseling
Definitions   Guidelines
Limitations   Summary
Background   References
Work Adjustment

PURPOSE OF THIS CHAPTER

T HE PURPOSE OF THIS paper is to offer recommendations for the use of group counseling in work adjustment for consideration by all persons concerned with adjustment to work. An effort was made to postulate some general guidelines in a "small group adjustment" approach, following an attempt at clarification of definitions and theoretical constructs related to work adjustment as an increasingly important component of the total rehabilitation process.

It is hoped that the schedule of activity suggested in this chapter can be of help to counselors and others in both public and private agencies burdened not only with the question of "what work adjustment *really* is", but also, "what are some techniques, methods, or approaches utilized in group counseling that might effect a more meaningful program of work adjustment for handicapped people?"

The results of a thorough study of the use of group counseling in work adjustment will enable administrators, counselors, and work adjustment personnel in their current efforts to (1) identify more clearly a definition of work adjustment as it relates to rehabilitation, (2) utilize small group techniques in the *modus operandi,* (3) evaluate existing programs, and (4) plan for the future development of new or extended work adjustment services for additional groups, i.e., the disadvantaged people in our society. In addition, this kind of pragmatic pursuit may succeed in stimulating more of our universities and colleges in establishing and maintaining training and research programs in the area of work adjustment.

DEFINITIONS

1. *Rehabilitation process:* consists of a planned, orderly sequence of services related to the total needs of the handicapped individual. It is concerned primarily with the handicapping problems resulting from disability rather than with the disability itself.

2. *Rehabilitation counseling:* the process in which the rehabilitation counselor or other professional person and handicapped client work in a face-to-face relationship in order for the client to move toward his best obtainable vocational, personal, and social adjustment.

3. *Joint rehabilitation programs:* those projects developed and operated jointly by departments of vocational rehabilitation and other state, county, or city units of government, including joint projects with private rehabilitation facilities.

4. *Disability:* a physical, mental, or social condition which materially limits, contributes to limiting, or if not corrected, will probably result in limiting an individual's activities or functioning. It includes behavioral disorders characterized by deviant social behavior or impaired ability to carry out normal relationships with family and community which may result from vocational, educational, cultural, social environment, and other factors.

5. *Work adjustment:* a treatment process utilizing work or aspects of work to modify behavior . . . it is not an evaluative process but is, as the words indicate, an adjustment or treatment process the objectives are to determine the success or failure of the adjustment plan and when to terminate the adjustment process (Hoffman, 1972).

6. *Prevocational evaluation:* this means the evaluation of such factors as activities of daily living, social development, and basic educational abilities (Hoffman, 1972).

7. *Work evaluation:* the assessment of vocational strengths and weaknesses through the utilization of work, real or simulated, for the purpose of developing a vocational plan of action (Hoffman, 1972).

8. *Group counseling in rehabilitation:* the process in which the counselor or therapist and a small group (8 to 10 members) of clients work together in order for the clients to acquire more normal develop-

mental trends and prepare for a more satisfying adjustment to life through productive activity—whether it is work for those with the potential of becoming employed, or to provide an opportunity for increasing self-actualization through a vocational type activity because of the severity of the disability, age, or other factors.

LIMITATIONS

In writing a chapter on the use of group counseling in work adjustment, an attempt has been made to be comprehensive and explicit in dealing with two areas of rehabilitation (i.e., work adjustment and group counseling); however, the sophistry surrounding both of these areas in the literature and the equivocation found in the practice of work adjustment produces a situation in which arbitrary decisions were required by the author in the descriptive statements on background, as well as in the final recommendation for an activity schedule. And, as a result, there are the more subtle limitations that may be present in any adumbration of suggestions and guidelines—those that derive from the need to depend on personal judgment and experience as to what is important or significant in making appropriate suggestions.

BACKGROUND

In the past decade, the public's interest and the professional's emphasis on vocational evaluation and work adjustment increased remarkably as a result of federal legislation in the 1960's; and, new demands and pressures felt by the vocational rehabilitation agencies and facilities as they attempted to serve new clients with new needs in a rapidly expanding state-federal program. In the early years, these new clients were, for the most part, mentally handicapped people— in more recent times, the greater concern for evaluation and work adjustment services has come because of the inclusion of people with socially handicapping conditions. At this point, most of the new program development for the socially handicapped person has taken place in the correctional field; however, some states have adopted rather broad guidelines for serving many people classified as disadvantaged.

It is obvious, in a review of current literature, that evaluation and work adjustment personnel will receive added demands to serve large numbers of disadvantaged people as a result of the proposed welfare reform measures—either by the Administration or by Congress. "This increase in the level of expectation for workshops and rehabilitation facilities will be a particularly challenging demand." (Hardy and Cull, 1972). A challenging demand not only in providing the new procedures, new programs, and facilities, but an even greater challenge is seen in the training of staff to provide effective work adjustment programs for large numbers of people in trouble in our society, either because of a physical or mental disability or because of poverty and its frightful consequences.

Professional workers in rehabilitation in the past who were interested in the area of work evaluation and adjustment to work received training either "on the job" or through short-term institutes in such facilities as the Institute for the Crippled and Disabled in New York City. In the late 1960's, graduate training programs were established in work evaluation and work adjustment at the University of Wisconsin-Stout, the University of Arizona, and Auburn University.

Work adjustment counselors or teachers have come from many related disciplines: occupational therapists, industrial arts teachers, rehabilitation counselors, and special education teachers; and, many have come from business, industry, or military administrative careers. In 1968, approximately ten years after the Rehabilitation Counseling Association was established as a division in the National Rehabilitation Association, the Vocational Evaluation and Work Adjustment Association was formed as a new division. Leaders in the new division acknowledged that the professional program would require a developmental approach in establishing a systematic body of knowledge which can be made relevant to work adjustment personnel (Nadolsky, 1971).

Assisting in the development of this new professional group, the Materials Development Center, University of Wisconsin-Stout, initiated a materials program in the field of work evaluation and work adjustment and has made a significant contribution in its distribution of such pamphlets and bulletins as *Suggested Publications for Developing an Agency Library on Work Evaluation and Work Adjustment*, printed in March, 1972.

WORK ADJUSTMENT

The work adjustment process is neither a new term nor an entirely new program in the field of rehabilitation. However, this aspect of the rehabilitation process continues to be misunderstood by administrators and misinterpreted by many practitioners. As Hoffman says in a recent paper, "Work adjustment, a treatment process utilizing work or aspects of work to modify behavior, is also at times defined as an evaluative process. It is not an evaluative process but is, as the words indicate, an adjustment or treatment process" (Hoffman, 1972). It is important to recognize this difference, and to acknowledge that the goals of work adjustment differ from evaluative and diagnostic activities. Hoffman continues in his paper, "In work adjustment, the objectives are to determine the success or failure of the adjustment plan and to determine when to terminate the work adjustment process. Prevocational, vocational, and work evaluation are assessment processes, and work adjustment (while evaluation does take place during the process) is a treatment process" (Hoffman, 1972).

Gefland sees work adjustment as "the next logical step" in the work evaluation procedure:

> Work adjustment, then, is an intensified continuation of the process of work evaluation. It utilizes such principles as (1) sharing the diagnosis with the disabled client, i.e., bringing to his attention his positive and negative work habits and attitudes through the observation of work behavior as manifested by his production of work and his behavioral approach to work, (2) working through faulty work patterns through consistent interpretation of them, (3) offering encouragement to improve poor habits, and (4) providing rewards when improvement occurs (Gefland, 1966).

The staff of the Work Adjustment Project at the University of Minnesota define work adjustment somewhat differently in a rather bold effort to provide a theory of work adjustment.

> "Work adjustment is defined as a function of the degree of correspondence (agreement) between an individual and his work environment. The individual brings to the job certain occupational abilities and vocational needs (preferences for specific reinforcing or rewarding conditions in jobs). The job, in turn, has certain ability requirements and offers opportunities for workers to gain specific reinforcers (e.g., money, social status, and security). The level of correspondence between the abilities of the individual and the ability requirements of his job is referred to as 'Satisfactoriness'. The level of correspondence between the vocational

needs (preference) of an individual and the reinforcer systems of his job is referred to as 'Satisfaction' . . ."

Satisfaction and Satisfactoriness are both related to tenure (remaining on a job or in an occupation). If satisfactoriness is sufficiently low, the worker is fired or demoted. If satisfaction is sufficiently low, the worker will quit the job. The statement of this theory or definition of work adjustment is clear and parsimonious and appears to provide one base in the establishment of what Lofquist calls a "tentative frame of reference". In his book, *Adjustment to Work,* Lofquist provides a thorough and comprehensive review of this theory developed by the staff of the Work Adjustment Project at Minnesota. (Lofquist, 1969).

John G. Cull, has suggested certain steps in the total work evaluation and work adjustment area which offer additional help in distinguishing the various activities of the process. Three steps are listed:

1. *Prevocational evaluation*—an activity which provides the very basic behaviors for an individual to be a member of our culture, e.g., personal grooming, eating, and other activities of daily living, etc.

2. *Work adjustment*—an activity in which the client begins to focus on general work skills and begins to learn the necessary work habits relative to attendance, punctuality, employer-employee relationships and employee-employee relationships—those activities that are common to all jobs.

3. *Work evaluation*—this step follows a decision which is made after the work adjustment program has ended: whether the client has the potential and the appropriate motivation to move into the world of work; or because of severity of disability, will become active in an "activity center" type program established to provide opportunities for maximum fulfillment by the individual short of placement in productive work.

Cull suggests that a work evaluation program will offer, at this point, an opportunity for evaluation or adjustment training in the specific skills and in a more reality-oriented approach in terms of job-tryouts, etc. It is at this point that the client begins to move toward vocational placement (Cull, 1972).

In reviewing statements by leaders in the field, it is clear that, while some confusion does exist in definition and description, all appear to be in agreement with Hoffman that work adjustment is a distinctive maneuver in the total evaluation and adjustment plan for the handicapped person and that work adjustment training is a "treatment process utilizing work or aspects of work to modify behavior" (Hoffman, 1972).

These various definitions and theoretical concepts are, all to some degree, relying on a type of behavior modification program which has become prevalent in many of the work adjustment training centers. Since this chapter is concerned with a different approach to treatment in the work adjustment process (i.e., group counseling), a history and description of behavior modification cannot be treated adequately here. However, it is important that rehabilitation personnel become knowledgeable in this emerging rehabilitation technique in the area of work adjustment. Recently, *Rehabilitation Tomorrow,* a research digest published by the West Virginia Research and Training Center, gave a brief description or definition of behavior modification for rehabilitation workers: "It implies increasing or decreasing the likelihood of a given behavior as a result of the pleasant or unpleasant consequences of that behavior. That is, positive or negative reinforcement following a response tends to increase the probability of that response, while punishment following a response tends to decrease the probability that it will be done again" (May, 1972). Research reports in this field indicate some rather dramatic results especially for severely handicapped people who were never able to respond in a positive way to traditional counseling and teaching methods. Some of the more important research findings in the field of work adjustment and rehabilitation are summarized briefly in this research release from the project in West Virginia.

GROUP COUNSELING

Walter Neff, in his book, *Work and Human Behavior,* chronicles the shift in work adjustment techniques from "guidance" to "counseling" in more recent times as rehabilitation staff have turned to the problems of the more severely handicapped person, which Neff states

". . . implies an increasing belief that the problems of adjustment to work are in some sense or other, problems of personality. Where these problems are severe, they cannot be solved by the giving of occupational information or the administration of tests. Some type of reconstruction of relevant areas of the personality appears to be required. The result has been an increasingly intensive search for appropriate methods of treatment" (Neff, 1968).

One method found appropriate in this search is group counseling, which was defined earlier in this chapter for rehabilitation purposes as the process in which the rehabilitation worker and a small group of clients work together in order for the clients to acquire more normal developmental trends and prepare for a more satisfying adjustment to life through productive activity.

Group counseling is becoming ubiquitous in many of the rehabilitation facilities and in many of the joint rehabilitation programs in communuities throughout the country. The procedures or techniques used in these group counseling sessions range from large groups (resembling classrooms), participating in problem solving and task oriented assignments with the work adjustment person viewed as an authority person—a teacher, a director of personnel, etc. to the small group approach based on Carl Rogers' basic encounter groups or other small group activities based exclusively in the affective area, with the work adjustment person acting as a group leader or facilitator who uses an extremely non-directive or group centered attitude as well as technique (Rogers, 1970). It seems important at this point to indicate certain references which will include a more comprehensive description of the great variety of small group treatment methods now being used. The T-Group or sensitivity training method developed by the National Training Laboratory in Bethel, Maine; the Basic Encounter group approach established at the Center for Studies of the Person at La Jolla, California; Rational-Emotive marathon groups developed by Albert Ellis's institute in New York City; Big Sur, California's Esalen Institute; and, other small group approaches are described in the following books:

The Theory and Practice of Group Psychotherapy, Irwin D. Yalom, Basic Books, Inc., New York, 1969.

T-Group Theory and Laboratory Method, John Wiley and Sons, New York, 1964.

Carl Rogers on Encounter Groups, Carl Rogers, Harper and Row, New York, 1970.

Group Counseling, Merle M. Ohlsen, Holt, Rinehard and Winston, New York, **1970.**

Two reasons for the emergence of this group counseling method in many of the work adjustment programs are (1) the lack of staff to serve the larger number of severely handicapped people—the economic situation, and (2) the prolific research writings in social psychology (and, its massive distribution to the public and professionals in educational settings) which indicates people can learn more about themselves and learn how to relate better to other people through the small group approach, thus becoming "ready" for a change in behavior in activities outside the group (Cartwright and Zander, 1960).

As Walter Neff states, "One of the major requirements of the adjustment to work is the ability to interact in certain appropriate ways with other people present on the scene." (Neff, 1968). No rehabilitation worker with experience in job placement and follow-up activities will argue with this statement.

Perhaps this thought as expressed by Neff can provide rehabilitation workers with the best rationale for the use of small groups in work adjustment training for handicapped people. Existentialism appears to provide the philosophical base for this "interaction with others on the scene" concept expressed by Neff. For example, in almost all of the group counseling techniques there is the use of an ahistorical approach (the "here and now" from Fritz Perls' Gestalt movement); participants are encouraged to interact on a feeling level, in an honest and open way—giving and receiving "feedback"; and, the reliance on the climate of, and even the "personality" of the group for pressures to change rather than an authoritative pressure for the "right or wrong" way. Arbuckle defines the existential psychologist's goal as one

> to help the individual achieve a state of acceptance, of responsibility for self, thus to be free . . . Man is free—he is what he makes of himself, the "outside" limites and restricts [e.g., a handicapping condition], but it does not determine [completely] one's way of life. Existence precedes essence . . . Man is not static, but he is rather in a constant state of growing, evolving, becoming. He is in a state of being, but also non-being . . . Existentitalism sees counseling and psychotherapy as primarily human encounter . . . The stress is on today rather than yesterday or tomorrow. A real human encounter must be in terms of now, and life and living are in terms of what is, not what was or what might be (Arbuckle, 1970).

Another hint of the origin of this philosophy base can be seen in

Rollo May's statements, "Therapy is concerned with helping the person experience his existence as real . . . which includes becoming aware of his potentialities and becoming able to act on the basis of them." (see Cull's statement referred to earlier). May continues,

> The significance of commitment is not that it is simply a vaguely good thing or ethically to be advised. It is a necessary prerequisite rather for seeing truth . . . decision precedes knowledge. We have worked normally on the assumption that, as the patient gets more and more knowledge and insight about himself, he will make appropriate decisions. This is a half truth. The second half of the truth is generally overlooked, namely, that the person cannot permit himself to get insight or knowledge until he is *ready* to decide, takes a decisive orientation to life, and has made the preliminary decision along the way (May, 1958).

There is no question that personnel working in work adjustment training for severely handicapped people can benefit from a thorough study of an existentialist psychology as expressed by Rollo May and others. The concepts reinforce the choice of group counseling since it appears that group work enables the client to have an opportunity to interact with other handicapped people in order to become "better adjusted to life and work".

GUIDELINES

The following guidelines relative to the use of group counseling in work adjustment are offered as tentative and temporary suggestions. It is hoped that the preceding background and review data itself will emphasize to the reader the limitations, restrictions, and barriers in establishing a well conceived academic supposition that can be followed as gospel and truth and also fit every situation. However, it is hoped that the guidelines can stimulate rehabilitation administrators, counselors, and work adjustment personnel in all areas to take a new look at what we call "group counseling", and examine carefully definitions and descriptions of what we call "work adjustment".

A quote from John Gardner's book, *No Easy Victories,* comes to mind as we look for specific guidelines for practicing group counseling in the work adjustment process:

> Our society must have the wisdom to reflect and the fortitude to act. It must provide the creative soil for new ideas and the skill and patience and hardihood to put those ideas into action (Gardner, 1968).

Activity Schedule

(Suggested guidelines for action—to be modified to the reality of each work situation. The plan should be viewed by the group leader as a flexible guide and *not* a formal schedule that has the blessing of research findings as "best way". Also, this schedule will require a great deal of modification to accommodate the work adjustment needs of people who are severely mentally retarded or who have other disabling conditions which would prevent them from participating in either the "encounter" approach or the "problem solving" sessions).

I. Introduction

   A. The work adjustment counselor or teacher arranges for eight to ten clients to meet in a small group setting (including individual conferences as scheduled). One hour per week for the group counseling and thirty minutes to one hour per individual session should be set up—this allows for eight weeks of one hour group counseling sessions and two weeks for personal interviews (see outline below).

   B. The work adjustment counselor interviews each client selected for the program *before* the ten week schedule begins. Participants are told in this conference about the overall plan for the group and individual meetings, the meeting place, time, others involved, and the specific reason for the use of the group approach. Each client has an opportunity to clarify for himself the purpose of the small group work and the work adjustment counselor will be able to gather new data about the individual which may help to facilitate the client's learning about himself in relation to the world of work.

   C. Also, before initiating the schedule, the work adjustment person should inform all administrators and colleagues of the plan and have copies of the schedule of activities distributed to other members of the staff. It is important for the work adjustment counselor to make clear the need for his remaining confidential in regard to the group sessions and to explain the importance of this "keeping quiet" attitude until each client, with the assistance of the group leader, prepares and distributes a progress report on himself to all staff, other agency professional staff, or to employers (at the end of the sessions).

D. One final activity is suggested for the facilitator prior to implementing the ten week activity schedule: (The term facilitator will be used for the work adjustment staff member during the remainder of this schedule). This final preliminary action will require that the facilitator schedule a one hour meeting of all participants (this follows the individual conferences). The purpose of this meeting is to teach clients what group counseling is: to review the schedule, to give an explanation of what is expected by participants, and what role or roles the facilitator will play. If video-tape or audio-tape is being considered for use in the groups, it may be wise for the facilitator to receive a group consensus on this as well as other technical matters. In this initial meeting, the group members are receiving instruction from the facilitator, and the climate should resemble an "open classroom" session. If honesty and openness is to come later, it's extremely important that the facilitator be honest about the purpose: "It's to help you adjust to work", for example. Also, the facilitator should share with the group all the "secrets and mysterious things" about group dynamics which he or she has learned (dependent in degree, of course, on the ability of clients to understand). Every effort should be made to avoid burdening the group members with the facilitator's problem of "wearing two hats". The facilitator is encouraged to say that "sometimes I will be there as your counselor, and I will do most of the listening in order for you to speak and listen to each other. Later, I will be a more active participant as we begin to work on specific problems regarding adjustment to work." And, of course, the facilitator should inform the clients of his own pledge of confidentiality. This informal meeting of the group should provide the facilitator with additional background information about individuals to plan selection of materials, etc. And last, it is important for the facilitator to avoid during the meeting a manipulative approach—be honest. For example, if direction is needed in your judgment, give it, but, watch for and avoid the more subtle "guarded and hidden" manipulative stance.

II. Small Group Activity—Phase I

(first four weeks—one hour per session in group counseling)

An opportunity is provided for clients to follow the basic encounter approach in group work—for each client to develop
interpersonal skills with others, with the facilitator encouraging
clients to be sensitive to feelings and to speak openly about
them. Certain exercises from books on encounter work, cassette
tapes, etc., may be helpful to establish early a climate of trust
and openness in this phase. The facilitator may recall exercises
or games used by his group in sensitivity or encounter experiences. Clients are encouraged to stay with the "here and
now" attitude within the group. The facilitator can assist the
group in looking at strengths rather than weaknesses.

Successful group counseling in this first four week period would mean
that each client experiences:

> greater acceptance of his total being—emotional, intellectual, and
> physical—as it *is,* including its potential . . . [appreciate that] indi-
> viduals can hear each other, can learn from another, such that each
> individual learns how he appears to others and what impact he has
> in interpersonal relationships . . . [that] the learnings in the group
> experience tend to carry over, temporarily or more permanently in re-
> lationships with [others in different settings] (Rogers, 1970).

III. Individual Counseling Sessions—Phase II

(one week for personal interviews between the facilitator and
individual clients—thirty minutes to one hour)

This week of individual conferences can be viewed as a bridge between the more "affective" area of group work which was experienced
in the four week encounter sessions and the more "cognitive" area of
group work which will be emphasized in the four problem solving
group sessions to follow. There are two major purposes for these interviews which interrupt the group counseling sessions: (1) the client
has an opportunity to share privately any feelings and concerns about
his experience in the earlier group sessions—he may feel uncomfortable
or embarrassed about his "openness" or that of others. (2) the client
has the opportunity to share privately any new ideas he may have
about himself or his adjustment to work. Also, the facilitator at this
point can briefly review plans for the more structured, problem solving

group sessions and, in some cases, he may assign a task for the client to work out prior to or during the group counseling.

(Perhaps this is a good place to interject some assumptions which are made by this author: (1) that the facilitator has received some basic training in group leadership, has participated himself in a sensitivity or encounter session, and has a clear understanding of the need for caution in this area. (2) that the facilitator is familiar with research findings which indicate that *all* people do not benefit from the basic encounter group nor other group counseling approaches, and that the literature shows none of the experienced and well-trained facilitators who feel that all group sessions are "successful" by whatever criteria they may be using, and that a small minority of people who engage in group counseling have experienced some harmful effects).

IV. Small Group Activity—Phase III

(for the next four weeks—one hour per session in group counseling)

The purpose of Phase III in this activity schedule for use of group counseling in work adjustment is to begin to focus on general work skills that are common to all jobs. The tasks to be assigned to the group will relate to learning ways of becoming effective workers in the real world of work. Some of the assignments made by the facilitator in these four more cognitive or task-oriented sessions will include:

(Note: this schedule for Phase III is set up to allow the facilitator to use the one hour group counseling session each week for each of the four suggestions that follow.)

A. Suggestion 1
   Assignment:

Each group member will share with the group the problems that he is experiencing in whatever work situation in which he has been involved, either in prevocational or work evaluation settings or job-tryouts, etc. These problems may have to do with attitudes toward employers, fellow employees, work habits, and other basic problems involved with any work setting. "Feedback" from others will be the key in these sessions.

B. Suggestion 2
   Assignment:

Each client will share with the group his own self-evaluation. A form can be devised by the facilitator to ask for a listing of strengths and weaknesses, including a statement at the end such as "What I can do to build on my strengths, and find ways to eliminate or accept my weaknesses in order to become free as a productive worker."

C. Suggestion 3
   Assignment:

Each client will share with the group *a plan* he has set up by himself or with his counselor (the facilitator, perhaps) for assuming responsibility for working. This may include getting a job, a job-tryout, an on-the-job experience, or some kind of vocational training program.

D. Suggestion 4
   Assignment:

Each client will be asked to share his evaluation of the group experience and the facilitator will encourage him to share his thoughts and feelings about himself and his future. The facilitator should encourage each client to express his feelings about future needs related to work adjustment.

V. Individual Counseling Sessions—Phase IV

   (one week for personal interviews between the facilitator and individual clients—thirty minutes to one hour)

In an attempt to integrate the group counseling method into the total work evaluation and work adjustment program, this last week of the activity schedule is designed to provide an opportunity for the work adjustment person to have an individual conference with each member of the group. The results of this interview will constitute a "joint communiqué" type of progress report in which the client and the work adjustment counselor sit down together and work out a report to be distributed to staff members and others who might be concerned with the client's work adjustment. This report can be made in the form of a recommendation, e.g., "It is recommended that this client participate in additional work adjustment programs; or, enter an activity type program not involved with competitive employment; or take vocational training; or, become employed."

This completes the suggested activity schedule. Activities that are involved with the feelings of clients and those that are emphasizing thoughts that will lead to action are viewed as a blending of these two areas (affective and cognitive) which will provide an opportunity for the handicapped person to learn better how to adjust to the world of work. George Isaac Brown in his introduction to *Confluent Education* defines this blending as follows:

> Confluent education is the term for the integration or flowing together of the affective and cognitive elements in individual and group learning —sometimes called humanistic or psychological education . . . a philosophy and a proess of learning in which the affective domain and the cognitive doman flow together, like two streams merging into one river, and are thus integrated in individual and group learning . . . It should be apparent that there is no intellectual learning without some sort of feeling, and there are no feelings without the mind's being somehow involved (Brown, 1971).

SUMMARY

An attempt was made to provide a brief background in two fields: work adjustment and group counseling; and, to specify a procedure for using group counseling methods in a work adjustment setting. This procedure takes the form of an activity schedule which should be viewed as a tentative guideline in helping handicapped people toward a better life through productive work.

REFERENCES

Allen, C. Thomas, Innovations in vocational evaluation and work adjustment. *Vocational Evaluation and Work Adjustment Bulletin, 4:*31-33, December, 1971.

Arbuckle, Dugald S.: *Counseling: Philosophy, Theory and Practice.* Boston, Allyn and Bacon, 1970.

Brown, George Isaac: *Human Teaching for Human Learning, An Introduction to Confluent Education.* New York, Viking Press, 1971.

Bulletins. Materials Development Center, The Department of Rehabilitation and Manpower Services, School of Education, University of Wisconsin—Stout, Menomonie, Wisconsin.

Cartwright, D., and Zander, A. (Eds.): *Group Dynamics: Research and Theory,* 2nd ed. Evanston, Row, Peterson and Company, 1960.

Cull, John G.: Statements made during a personal interview at his office at the Virginia Commonwealth University Regional Counselor Training Program, Woodrow Wilson Rehabilitation Center, Fishersville, Virginia, August 3, 1972.

Cull, John G., and Hardy, Richard E.: The role of the rehabilitation facility in the evaluation of the welfare recipient. In Hardy, Richard E., and Cull, John G. (Eds.): *Work Evaluation for Rehabilitation Services,* Springfield, Thomas, 1972.

Gardner, John W.: *No Easy Victories.* New York, Harper and Row, 1968.

Gefland, Bernard: The concept of reality as used in work evaluation and work adjustment. *Journal of Rehabilitation,* November-December: 26-28, 1966.

Hoffman, Paul R.: Work evaluation: An overview. Unpublished paper presented as Chapter I for a book on work evaluation in rehabilitation by Hardy, Richard E., and Cull, John G., in press.

Lofquist, Lloyd, and Dawis, Rene V.: *Adjustment to Work.* New York, Appleton-Century Crofts, 1969.

May, Rollo: Contributions of existential psychotherapy. *Existence,* New York, Simon and Schuster, 1958.

Nadolsky, Julian M.: Patterns of consistency among vocational evaluators. *Vocational Evaluation and Work Adjustment Bulletin,* 4:13-25, December, 1971.

National Training Laboratory: *T-Group Theory and Laboratory Method.* New York, Wiley and Sons, 1964.

Neff, Walter S.: *Work and Human Behaior.* New York, Atherton Press, 1968.

Ohlsen, Merle M.: *Group Counseling.* New York, Holt, Rinehart, and Winston, 1970.

Rehabilitation Tomorrow. West Virginia Research and Training Center Institute, West Virginia, *Vol. 2,* May, 1972.

Rogers, Carl R.: *Carl Rogers on Encounter Groups.* New York, Harper and Row, 1970.

Yalom, Irwin D.: *The Theory and Practice of Group Psychotherapy.* New York, Basic Books, 1969.

INDEX

163